NAMING GOD TODAY

NAMING GOD TODAY

Edited by

H.-E. MERTENS and L. BOEVE

LEUVEN
UNIVERSITY PRESS

UITGEVERIJ PEETERS
LEUVEN

1994

ANNUA NUNTIA LOVANIENSIA
XXXVIII

CIP KONINKLIJKE BIBLIOTHEEK ALBERT I, BRUSSEL

ISBN 90 6186 614 6 (Leuven University Press)
D/1994/1869/33
ISBN 90 6831 603 6 (Uitgeverij Peeters)
D/1994/0602/63

© Leuven University Press / Presses Universitaires de Louvain
Universitaire Pers Leuven
Krakenstraat 3, B-3000 Leuven (Belgium)

Uitgeverij Peeters, Bondgenotenlaan 153, B-3000 Leuven (Belgium)

TABLE OF CONTENTS

Frontispiece: Photograph B. Willaert (J. Jans)

HOMAGE B. WILLAERT

On the first of October 1992, Professor Benjamin Willaert became "honorary ordinary professor". He was born in Izenberge, West-Flanders, on 24 October 1926. After his ordination and a short teaching appointment in an episcopal college, he became professor of dogmatic theology at the Diocesan Seminary in Bruges in 1955. In addition, he was for many years the "provisor" of the seminary, responsible for its material management. In these two rather divergent functions, which he combined successfully, he provided for generations of seminarians both spiritual and material sustenance.

In 1969, on the occasion of the reorganization of the Faculty of Theology in the autonomous "Katholieke Universiteit te Leuven", Benjamin Willaert was appointed professor of Dogmatic Theology in both the Flemish and the English speaking programs. His field of specialization was Special Dogmatic Theology. The students in the first cycle enjoyed his courses on Christology and Creation and Eschatology, whereas the second cycle students could take "special questions". For several years, these "special questions" concentrated on Friedrich Schleiermacher's writings. In addition he taught readings of modern theological texts and lectured on the history of modern theology. His main interest has always been the basic question of belief in God. As the first chairman of the dogmatic research department and as chairman of the teaching committee for the Programs in English, he contributed in many ways to assure the quality of the Faculty.

Professor Willaert has been a faithful colleague, never escaping his duty by absenteeism. Concentration on special dogma did not exclude any other topic from his broad interest because *nihil humanum* could ever be *alienum* to his vivid mind. His mastery of languages, his personal wit, his relativizing humor, his warm heart and delicate respect for people and, above all, his deep religious concern to safeguard authentic faith in God and Christ brought him general trust and esteem among professors and students.

In popular usage, the word "dogmatic" may have a somewhat negative connotation. "Dogmatic" means then: predetermined and authoritarian concepts and therefore lack of freedom in thinking, a biased approach to reality and closed-mindedness. If that were the only possible meaning of "dogmatic", then the dogmatician Willaert would have to be called "undogmatic". Indeed, far from proclaiming postulates or simply repeating preconceived formulas, he constantly stimulated the students to see the complexity of the truth, reminding them that every statement could be questioned in an intelligent way with a view to discovering the part of truth hidden in its opposite. When the students asked him one day why he did not discuss the "burning issues", he replied that there was in his opinion only one burning issue in theology: hell...! He was indeed convinced that so-called "burning issues" are often inflated transitory ideas and transient fashionable concerns, which inhibit reflection on the basic issues, while they give the comfortable illusion of being courageously engaged in the heart of the matter. By shaking the naive confidence in simplistic slogans, fixed formulas and "ephemeral" topics, he has been an "eye-opener" for those who were prepared and able to follow his highly refined "free-wheeling" through the dogmatic landscape.[1]

I trust that the retirement of our colleague will not deprive the young staff of his wise advise. May we hope that Benjamin Willaert will use the sea of time now available to write down his personal views on basic theological problems? The new generations of students, who will not enjoy his *viva vox* in class, will then have the opportunity to profit from the personal approach of this original thinker. Might not this reading open their eyes and stimulate them to reply critically in their turn: "Yes, but is not the opposite also true in a way?" I wholeheartedly wish colleague Willaert *ad multos annos*.

Joël Delobel
Dean

---

1. The doctoral dissertations and licentiate theses, directed by B. Willaert, are listed on the following pages.

DISSERTATIONS AND THESES
DIRECTED BY B. WILLAERT

Doctorate in Sacred Theology (S.T.D.)

BACKIANADAN, Joseph Francis
'Love for God and Fellowmen' in the Life and Works of Mahatma Gandhi
   1989, XX-271 p.

DE BARY, Edward Oscar
Christ, Cosmos and Change: A Study of the Relationship of Christology and Cosmology
   1983, XLII-602 p.

GICHURE, Peter I.
Contextual Theology: A Contribution to Theological Method
   1992, XLIV-365 p.

HALL, Douglas C.
Participated Trinitarian Relations: Dialectics of Method, Understanding, and Mystery in the Theology of Thomas Aquinas
   1988, LXIV-1718 p.

MERRIGAN, Terrence
'A Theology of the Religious Imagination': Faith and Reason in the Life and Work of John Henry Newman
   1989, CVII-381 + 66 + 250 p.

STEEN, Marc
Het actuele thema van de lijdende God. Vooronderstellingen, illustratie en evaluatie van recent theopaschitisme
   1990, LI-449 p.

VAN DER VLOET, Johan
De christen aan het einde van de moderniteit. De bijdrage van Romano Guardini tot een theologische kritiek van de moderniteit
   1989, XLVII-436 p. (Co-director: I. Verhack)

Ph.D. in Religious Studies

KENZIG, Stephen R.
Toward a Theology of the Symbol: Representational Symbols and the Christian Community
   1985, XLVII-420 p.

LAU, Stephen L.
Faith and the Human Condition: Paul Tillich's Politicization of Theology
1982, LXX-377 p.

MERKLE, John
The Genesis of Faith in the Dept Theology of Abraham Joshua Heschel
1982, XV-583 p.

NASH, Richard T.
Job's Misconception: A Critical Analysis of the Problem of Evil in the
Philosophical Theology of Charles Hartshorne
1992, IV-211 p.

Licentiate in Sacred Theology (S.T.L.)

ASSENGA, Faustini M.A.
God with us: Aquinas' and Rahner's Views as a Preliminary to Some
African Christian Approaches
1992, XIV-116 p.

CEUNEN, Wim
De theologie van de rechtvaardiging bij Gasparo Contarini (1483-1542)
1992, XXIII-126 p.

DEMOLDER, Jozef
Gods handelen als taalgebeuren: een studie van de hermeneutische theologie van Gerhard Ebeling
1982, XIX-186 p.

EMENOGU, Alexander
Christian Conversion and Religious Commitment
1992, XXII-115 p.

KANJIRATHINGAL, Davis
'Potentia oboedientialis': Anthropological-Theological Premise to Karl
Rahner's Theology of Incarnation
1976, XXVI-213 p.

KENIS, Leo
Lijdensgeschiedenis en messiaanse herinnering: over de receptie van
Walter Benjamin in de hedendaagse theologie
1982, XX-161 p.

KRIKILION, Walter
Gods onveranderlijkheid en veranderlijkheid in de menswording vanuit
de visie van Karl Rahner. Een hedendaagse theologische verantwoording
1987, XXXV-155 p.

MIRAS, Joseph A.
Doing Theology in the Philippines: a Study on the Theological Methods of Selected Filipino Contemporary Theologians
1991, XXI-137 p.

MKHATSHWA, Smangaliso P.
Modern Anthropology in 'Gaudium et spes': Post-Vatican II Perspectives
1973, XXVI-129 p.

NEVEN, Emile
Naar zijn beeld en gelijkenis: het mysterie van Gods immanentie in de concrete menselijke natuur
1975, XII-61 + 153 p.

VANDEPITTE, Beny
God en het verlangen van de vervreemde mens
1992, XVIII-134 p.

VAN ISEGHEM, Mieke
De invloed van het kerkelijk standpunt op de beeldende kunst. Een dogmatisch-historische studie
1990, XXIV-131 p. + Appendix.

VANLANDUYT, Koen
Een vergelijkende studie in de proces-christologie. De proces-christologie bij J.B. Cobb, Jr, D.R. Griffin, S.M. Ogden
1986, XXVI-128 p.

VAN STEENDAM, Guido
De nacht van duizend-en-één verhalen: een oriëntatie bij de narratieve theologie
1978, XVIII-154 p.

WALSH, Joseph
Logos and Process: the Christology of John B. Cobb
1979, XXI-136 p.

WULLEPIT, Antoon
Grondelementen tot een theonome antropologie: een studie van het mensbeeld in P. Tillich's systematische theologie
1978, XII-123 p.

NAMING GOD TODAY
AND THE THEOLOGICAL PROJECT OF
PROF. DR. BENJAMIN WILLAERT

The one that alone is wise
does not want and still wants to be named God
HERACLEITOS

In March 1993, the Faculty of Theology (K.U. Leuven) organized a colloquium in honor of Em. Prof. Dr. B. Willaert. The title of the colloquium, 'Naming God Today', could not have been better, for the investigation of the conditions in the naming of God has a central place in the thinking of B. Willaert. What can we say about God? What can we call God? How can we say something about God? And in the perspective of these questions, what is the object of theo-logy? What is its function and what are the conditions for a healthy theological approach? Under B. Willaert, these questions point to a radicalized theological hermeneutics.

The starting-point is essential for the radicality of theological hermeneutics. Each time we attempt to say something about God, or about God's action in the world, we fail. The reality we name God cannot be put into words. All of what we say about God is always too much and not enough: too much because we cannot grasp the divine reality in words and not enough because that reality is always more and transcends whatever is said about it. But even if all our words for God are incompetent to name Him, Her, or It – and we know that our attempts to name necessarily do not succeed – we cannot stop naming God; we feel compelled to do it.

The use of words to refer to the referent of 'God' was the problematic of B. Willaert's valedictory lecture entitled 'Daring and Humbleness in the Naming of God'. 'Humbleness' stands for the attitude of openness and receptivity to, and the feeling of dependence on, the mystery that carries us and which we call 'God'. In this perspective, 'daring' cannot be correctly understood other than as 'daring out of humbleness'. The humbleness not only questions all talk about God – and silences the one who opens oneself to the mystery – but also forces that one to speak, to witness to the mystery. One dares to name God because one feels oneself forced to do it. Humbleness leads, at the same time, to silence and to witnessing. This attitude of receptive openness, standing in the openness, and witnessing to the mystery that enters the openness, is fundamental to every theological activity. The encounter with the unnameable urges both respect for the 'unnameability' of what is encountered and the witness to it. In three sections, Willaert elaborated this problematic. We briefly develop them here below. Evoking Augustine's attitude towards the mystery to which he devoted his 'Confessions', Willaert first sketched the fundamental condition of the believer, of the one who dares to name God. In a second section, with reference to Thomas Aquinas, he examined the question of the possibility to name God. He concluded with some reflections on this enigma: whenever we name God, we make a God for ourselves, but knowing this must not prevent us from looking for words to witness to God.

One of the most nuanced evocations of the fundamental condition of the believer who wants to name and to praise one's God, is given by Aurelius Augustine: "You are great, Lord, and highly to be praised (Ps 47,2): great is your power and your wisdom is immeasurable (Ps 146,5). Man, a little piece of your creation, desires to praise you, a human being bearing his mortality with him (2 Cor 4,10), carrying with him the witness of his sin and the witness that you resist the proud (1 Pet 5,5). Nevertheless, to praise you is the desire of man, a little piece of your creation. You stir man to take pleasure in praising you, because you have made us for yourself, and our heart is restless until it rests in you. Grant me Lord to know and understand (Ps 118,34.73.144) which comes first - to call upon you or to praise you, and whether knowing you precedes calling upon you. But who calls upon you when he does not know you? For an ignorant person might call upon someone else instead of the right one. But surely you may be called upon in prayer that you may be known. Yet how shall they call upon him in whom they have not believed? and how shall they believe without a preacher? (Rom 10,14). They will praise the Lord who seek for him (Ps 21,27). In seeking him they find him, and in finding they will praise him. Lord, I would seek you, calling upon you - and calling upon you is an act of believing in you"[1]. In this text, the knowledge of God appears immediately in the context of praise and prayer. The naming of God finds its initial incentive in the encounter with the mystery that invites one to be its witness.

But our words for God do not succeed in representing what God is, what God is about. The consciousness that all talk about God has to be implemented in an attitude of knowing that no expression can contain God, can be found in the first chapters of Thomas Aquinas' *Summa theologiae*. In his five strategies to prove God's existence, Thomas concludes each time with expressions similar to the following: that which has been referred to in the exposition, we name God (e.g. 'et hoc dicimus Deum'[2]). Notable is the phrase 'we name'. Furthermore, using five different strategies, Thomas Aquinas proves God's existence (*Utrum Deus sit*), but afterwards, he questions any presupposed referent of God (*De*

---

1. AUGUSTINE, *Confessiones* I,1 (ed. The Fathers of the Church: a New Translation, 21, Washington, 1966, p. 2); for a similar evocation, see *Conf.* I,4. For Augustine, believers come to know God in the preaching of the Church, which offers them formulas to express their faith.

2. Thomas AQUINAS, *Summa Theologiae* 1a Q2 art3.

Dei simplicitate). Knowing *that* God exists, one should ask *how* God is in order to know *what* God is. To this Thomas advises the following procedure: first, we have to examine what God is not, second, how we can know God, and third, how we can name God.[3] All positive naming is preceded and accompanied by a negative movement. Believers and theologians always have to be aware of the fact that, in professing and explaining the faith, they use categories, images, and models that are not specific and adequate enough to signify the referent of God because these categories are taken from our vocabulary, which is more fit to express human conduct in the world and the things of the world. Therefore, those categories, images, and models only serve to refer to the referent of God when they are used within that consciousness of inadequacy. Because they fail in signifying the referent of God, they paradoxically succeed in referring to it.

But the fact that our words do not fit to describe the 'what' of God, may not prevent us from talking about God even if this would entail that we make a God for ourselves. There is no alternative: all naming suffers from an incurable lack of correspondence with that which calls to be named. Even if our images of God show a logical, esthetical, and ethical coherence, so much so that they seem consistent to us, there is *a priori* no evidence that they correspond to the reality of God. The contextuality of the naming of God necessarily leads to the fact that we create a God for ourselves. But as Kant wrote, we create a God for ourselves to honor the One who created us.[4] As long as we know what we are really doing when we refer to God, and are aware that our vocabulary is necessarily human and all-too-human, we honor God in naming God, for this naming is at the same time accompanied by a recognition of the 'unnameability' of what we 'name' 'God'.

As the context has an important role in the formation and significance of theological language, a change of context immediately affects the reference to the unnameable. Each generation and culture stands before the never-ending and never-completed task of looking for images and models suitable to name the mystery that enters the openness in themselves. As an old Hasidic tale tells: "The disciples ask their master why, since scripture is never redundant or uses unnecessary words, the Torah

3. Thomas AQUINAS, *Summa theologiae* 1a Q3.
4. Cfr. I. KANT, *Religion within the Limits of Reason Alone*, New York, 1960, pp. 156-157 (in Part Two: Concerning the pseudo-service of God in a statutory religion: 1. Concerning the universal subjective ground of the religious illusion). In the second edition Kant adds a footnote to the text: "for here we create a God for ourselves". Text of the footnote: "Though it does indeed sound dangerous, it is in no way reprehensible to say that everyman creates a God for himself, nay must make himself a God according to moral concepts (and must add those infinitely great attributes which characterize a Being capable of exhibiting in the world, an object commensurate to himself), in order to honor Him the One who created him".

says: 'The God of Abraham, the God of Isaac and the God of Jacob' rather than the simpler 'The God of Abraham, Isaac, and Jacob' — Because, the Master replies, each generation must enter anew into its covenant with God"[5].

This valedictory lecture of B. Willaert concluded the colloquium 'Naming God Today'. The other lectures are presented in this volume. After a preliminary text about today's insuperable hermeneutical condition of the theologian, the second article examines the validity and relevance of a panentheistic theology, and in contrast to this, the third article examines the necessity of a theology exclusively based on revelation. A final contribution attempts to transcend the dilemma between a panentheistic theology and a supernatural one by proposing a renewed alliance between revelatory theology and philosophy.

In the first article, Herman-Emiel Mertens sketches the actual *status questionis*. 'Re-Thinking "God" Today' contains a plea for a thoroughly hermeneutical approach to preserve the intelligibility and workability of our conceptions of God. The inherent difficulties, the doubts, and the uneasy quest for solutions cannot be excuses to abandon the hermeneutical task and to stick, as fundamentalists do, with an untranslated and literal vocabulary. The theologian has to look for a new, liberating language anchored in experience — a religious language that is capable of provoking a 'disclosure'.

Georges De Schrijver s.j. examines the influence of different cosmological reflections upon the conceptualization of the attributes of God in 'Changes in the Understanding of the Attributes of God in Deism, Newton, and Spinoza: The Influence of Cosmological Reflection on Religious Thought'. His starting-point is the deistic God-image of Leibniz and Descartes. This deistic God-clockmaker transcends the world. The attempt of Newton to retrieve the bond between God and the world failed. Spinoza, on the contrary, succeeded in this project. By 'naturalizing' God and concomitantly divinizing naturing nature, Spinoza is able to conceive the unique Substance under the attributes of both thought and extension: 'deus sive natura (naturans)'. Spinoza's reflections are certainly worthwhile if one wants to develop a cosmic religiosity in the context of the late twentieth century. This becomes more relevant nowadays in response to a new religious sensitivity appearing in the circles of cosmologists and natural scientists — a sensitivity that is often conceptualized in neo-deistic or neo-spinozistic God-vocabulary. With this in mind, De Schrijver inquires whether or not we are capable of finding points of contact with a modified spinozism for the development of a religious world-view adequate for our age — an endeavour exemplified by St. Thomas Aquinas, who in his time developed a relevant world-view

---

5. From H. KASIMOV, *No Religion is an Island, Abraham Joshua Heschel and Interreligious Dialogue,* New York, 1991, p. 117.

by appropriating and elaborating aristotelian cosmological thought.

The third essay, written by Antoon Vergote, is entitled 'Beyond the Seduction of Deism'. In sharp contrast to the preceding contribution, Vergote does not develop a critical assessment of deism, but opts for a confrontation with the deistic legacy. He considers deism a post-christian return to a form of natural religion, which radically contrasts with supernatural religion. Natural religion remains within the boundaries of human reason and experience. It distances itself explicitly from every form of religious authority, revelation, divine intervention and election, and an externally mediated salvation. But the personal God of Christianity is not a God of concepts but a God who can be met as a person. The Christian God reveals Himself in His Word as 'You', as love, and transcends the neutral God of deism. The attractiveness of deism for conceptualizing God, is due to the fact that the God of deism does not have to be considered as the Other, who breaks our self-enclosedness. Speaking and thinking about God not only has to deal with this seduction but even needs to go beyond it.

Finally, Theo de Boer discusses thoroughly the easily stated distinction between the God of the philosophers and the God of Pascal. In doing so, he implicitly tries to develop a reflection on the presuppositions of the contrast that has been revealed in the contributions of De Schrijver and Vergote. First, de Boer sketches the paradigm change in philosophy which occurred with the rise of historicism and the philosophy of life. This paradigm change supplies an opportunity for reconsidering the conflict between faith and reason. Therefore, de Boer pleads for a philosophy that handles the conceptualization, interpretation, and discussion of basic religious categories. This is the opening for a philosophical translation of religious wisdom. Christian theology and philosophy, still relevant in our days, have much at stake in the remembrance of the narrative foundation of wisdom, the reconstruction of the history of dogma, the re-thinking of central categories, and finally, a philosophical meta-reflection.

Speaking also for the co-editor, Prof. Dr. H.-E. Mertens, I want to offer my thanks to the 'Chair Mgr. A. Dondeyne', which co-sponsored the lecture of Prof. Dr. T. de Boer. We are also grateful to Dennis Gonzalez, Daniel Frett, Susan Roll, John Ries and Leo Kenis for their assistance as regards the translations. We also would like to thank the Dean of the Faculty of Theology, J. Delobel, the Fund for Publications (K.U. Leuven), and the person in charge of the series 'Annua nuntia', F. Neirynck, for offering the opportunity to publish the proceedings of the colloquium. We direct a final word of congratulations to Em. Prof. Dr. Benjamin Willaert and wish him all the best in his well deserved retirement.

Heirbaan 86   Lieven BOEVE
B-1745 Opwijk

RE-THINKING "GOD" TODAY

Do not be impulsive in speech,
nor be guilty of hasty utterance in God's presence.
God is in heaven and you are on earth,
so let your words be few.   *Eccles 5,2*

On April 15, 1989, the Free University of Amsterdam organized a workshop on the subject of "God" under the title, "Can you imagine everything when you say God?"[1]. That expression reminded me strongly of the way our colleague Benjamin Willaert proceeds in private conversations as well as in public discussions. With his eyes half closed, seemingly somewhat playful, yet in fact very seriously, he then usually asks: "Is it thinkable that...?". Hypothetical thinking suits him very well. The testing of different ways of thinking can, indeed, be extremely fruitful. But also with regard to the God problem? That is our question here.

What can you think about God? Can you imagine everything when you say God? However, 'can' is one thing, and 'may' is another. Hence the pertinent question: *"May you imagine everything when you say God?"*. From the viewpoint of religious studies, the first question is answered affirmatively. The second question alludes to a criterion, which includes, in a Christian perspective, the normative character of the Bible and tradition. Still, with that 'may', more is at stake. It has also to do with our contemporary cultural situation. Representations are so much products of time and space, that their significance and, hence, their practicability is conditioned by it. The God images of Christian theology must therefore be put to the test of both tradition and the present *Sitz im Leben*. This is a never ending quest, not only because our knowledge of God always remains incomplete, but also because the cultural context which includes the search for God is ceaselessly changing. "We see only puzzling reflections in a mirror (...). My knowledge now is partial" (1 Cor 13,12).

Needless to say, the God problem is at the center of the *whole* of theology. Moreover, it is the *conditio sine qua non* for defining every other theological problem. When Christology, pneumatology, ecclesiology, protology, the doctrine of grace, and eschatology neglect talking about God, they are not theology at all. "God" is *the* theme, on which the entire theological enterprise stands or falls. It is not merely a theoretical or an academic matter, but it touches the very existence of the (un)believer: one's mentality, ethical behavior, intercourse with others, prayer,

---

1. *Kun je je bij God alles voorstellen?* Verslagboek van een themadag, VUSA-centrum, Amsterdam, 1989.

spirituality, hope. Moreover, "God" is the centuries-old problem that occupies not only religions and churches, but philosophies and world views as well, from time immemorial up to the present.

One is never ready with it. No theologian will ever say the final word. No publication will put a definitive end to the discussion. It is an eternal starting-again, with regard to both the conceptual definition of the problem and the analysis of the current complex of questions. "Ut inventus quaeratur immensus est", wrote Augustine. God is so great that, once found, he still can be sought for. Moreover, because of fundamental changes of the cultural climate and radical shifts of the social order, all representations are in need of profound revision.

Nothing is More Difficult to Think

In his well-known proof of God's existence, Anselm of Canterbury defines God as "something above which nothing can be thought". But the highest which is thinkable is also the most difficult to think. Every thinking or speaking about God must take this into account. No problem is more complicated than the problem of "God". Everything that is said about God is only meaningful for convinced believers, and one believes more with the heart than with reason. Hans Küng rightly says: "It must be admitted that, in so far as they seek to prove something, the proofs of God are meaningless. But in so far as they bring God into the discussion, they are very meaningful. As definite answers they are inadequate, but as open questions they are irrecusable. There is no doubt that the *probative character of the proofs of God is finished* today, *but their content remains important"*[2].

In any case, not only God's existence is extremely problematic, but his essential nature as well. Even believers ask themselves: what do I say when I say "God"?

God is no object of empirical perception. We look at nature. But when we consider it as God's creation, we interpret our perception out of our belief in God. In Antony Flew's "parable of the two explorers in the jungle" who suddenly discover a well-kept flower-bed, the two assertions are false: the one made by the theist ("there is a gardener"), and the one made by the atheist ("there is none"). For God is no empirical datum. The immanent God is transcendent, unseen and invisible: "dwelling in unapproachable light; him no one has ever seen or can ever see" (1 Tim 6,16). Immediate contact is excluded. With the word "God" we reach the boundaries of our imagination. In addition, it is a limit concept. The unimaginable is the quasi unthinkable. Augustine already knew: "Si

---

2. H. KÜNG, *Does God Exist?*, Garden City, NY, 1980, p. 534. Cf. W. KASPER, *The God of Jesus Christ*, London, 1984, p. 12: "Proofs of God are usually convincing only to those wo already believe in God".

comprehendis non est Deus". If you understand it, it is not God. Or, as Gerhard Terstegen said: "Ein begriffener Gott ist kein Gott".

Since Kant and the Enlightenment, we have fully realized that God's existence can not be proven rationally (otherwise, all reasonable people could be convinced). But it can be accepted for practical reasons. Is it a wager with important ethical implications, though not totally irrational, something like "le pari de Pascal"? Yet, the gambling of the God-believer cannot bypass the identity question: "Who's who?".

Modesty suits everyone who thinks and speaks about God, philosopher and theologian alike. Besides, the concept of God is no invention of philosophers or theologians; it originated from the religious intuition and mythical speech of the primitive, religious person. Factual thinking and objectifying speech fail to grasp it. "Do not be impulsive in speech": the golden advice of Ecclesiastes is more than reasonable. It does not mean an oath of secrecy nor an approval *avant la lettre* of the well-known advice by Wittgenstein: "What we cannot speak about we must pass over in silence". No ban on speech, but an exhortation to utter cautiousness and modesty, since "every speech about a transcendent God is like dancing on a rope, with an abyss on both sides: anthropomorphism and agnosticism"[3]. A difficult task. In his recent commentary on the *Apostles' Creed*, Nicholas Lash writes: "There is nothing that may be easily said of God; if we find it easy to say certain things of God, the chances are, when we say them, we lose sight of God"[4].

The history of theology (and of the churches!) abundantly shows how often the word "God" has been misused. Martin Buber once rightly wrote: "What word of human speech is so misused, so defiled, so desecrated as this! All the innocent blood that has been shed for it has robbed it of its radiance. All the injustice that it has been used to cover has effaced its features. When I hear the highest called 'God', it sometimes seems almost blasphemous"[5]. A similar complaint is heard from Hans Küng in his recent commentary on the Creed: "Jedes Wort dieses Credo – vom Wort 'Ich glaube' und vom Wort 'Gott' angefangen – ist im Lauf der Jahrhunderte ja auch mißverstanden, mißbraucht, gar geschändet worden"[6]. Would we not rather prefer to keep silence? Not at all. We can nor may ignore the name. This is Buber's conclusion: "None has become so soiled, so mutilated. Just for this reason I may not abandon it"[7]. The whole question is: "what's in a name?".

3. W.A. DE PATER, *Taalanalytische perspectieven op godsdienst en kunst*, Antwerpen, 1970, p. 45.

4. N. LASH, *Believing Three Ways in One God*, London, 1992, p. 22.

5. M. BUBER, *Eclipse of God*, New Jersey, 1979, p. 7.

6. H. KÜNG, *Credo*, München-Zürich, 1992, p. 20.

7. M. BUBER, *Eclipse of God* (n. 5), p. 7.

Hermeneutics Wanted

The intelligibility and workability of our conceptions of God are dependent on a sound hermeneutics. From the theological point of view, it concerns the dialectics between the ancient text and a new interpretation. How to give an up to date interpretation of the original message: that is the ever reappearing question. How to re-translate the biblical and other traditional images of God within our contemporary culture: that is the never ending task of the theologian. Experience teaches how misleading fundamentalist and untranslated repetition of biblical quotations can be. In this case, the appeal to the saying "traduttore traditori" is a misleading alibi. An untranslated, literal reproduction of the ancient text can be a gross betrayal of its original meaning and intention. The formulation of old questions and old answers must be punctured so as to touch their real tenor. When the questions have become obsolete, then the answers usually lose their meaning as well. Nothing is as hollow and useless as an old-fashioned imagery that is totally passé.

Without propagating reckless iconoclasm, we must maintain that all the images of God, including the most traditional, even the biblical ones, must be subjected to a severe criticism. That does not mean that we must pull them down rashly and without mercy. By such vandalism nobody does well.

On the other hand, a clean up is required, for today we can no longer speak simplistically about God as the father, the almighty, the creator, the judge. "There are images that have had their day. Moreover, it is no longer possible to harden images into artificially maintained dogmas"[8]. Also the classic philosophical conceptions of (neo-)platonist and aristotelian signature must be called into question. The representations of God as the highest idea, the first cause, the unmoved mover, the absolute and necessary Being, perfection, final goal, have lost much of their expressiveness. If in 1994 one simply echoes Calvin or Jansenius when speaking about providence, election and predestination, one runs the risk of falling on deaf ears. But are not the deistic conceptions of the Enlightenment virtually surpassed as well?

Furthermore, is the term "God" itself still useful and meaningful in our post-modern time? This question is unavoidable. Some theologians make mention of the erosion of the Supreme Being and the end of metaphysical God-talk. Also of biblical speech?

Obviously, we are far removed from the patriarchal (and largely agrarian) culture of the Bible, the Church fathers and the medieval theologians. Their mythological language sounds so strange. In our modern and post-modern world, with its secularized culture, its longing for democracy and its holistic sensibility, we must rely on other images

8. O. JAGER, *Oude beelden spreken een nieuwe taal*, Baarn, 1990, p. 17.

and symbols. All images with alienating effects must be tabooed, since we can no more return beyond the criticism of God and religion by Feuerbach, Marx, Nietzsche and Freud.

A New, Liberating Language

The world belongs to the daring. The future of Christian theology lays largely in the hands of those theologians who are honest, courageous and inventive enough to forge a new language. A language wherein we understand God anew. A language wherein such old words as Promise, Future, Freedom no longer remain powerless. A language also with brand-new words which call forth values.

Why not, albeit by way of experiment, speak with Sallie McFague, about God as body (cosmic), as mother (for the feminine attributes), as lover, as friend[9]? The distant, unmoved, apathic God must yield pride of place for the immanent, sympathetic God: the ground of our being and our ultimate concern (P. Tillich), the powerless omnipotence (H. Berkhof), the (com)passionate God (D. Bonhoeffer), the crucified God (J. Moltmann), the "great companion – the fellow-sufferer who understands" (A.N. Whitehead), the fellow-fighter (liberation theologians). With Schillebeeckx we speak of "God's rule conceived in terms of humanity".

In his charismatic appeal for a religionless christianity, Dietrich Bonhoeffer has demonstrated that God as a stop-gap is played out in our emancipated world. No more *deus ex machina* at the boundaries of our existence, filling up the gaps in our knowledge and abilities. Bonhoeffer pleads for a secular interpretation of the biblical concepts: "The day will come when men will once more be called so to utter the word of God that the world will be changed und renewed by it. It will be a new language, perhaps quite non-religious, but liberating and redeeming – as was Jesus' language; it will shock people and yet overcome them by its power; it will be the language of a new righteousness and truth, proclaiming God's peace with men and the coming of his kingdom"[10].

A Language Anchored in Our Experience

The secularization of the human person is an irreversible historical fact. According to the Dutch theologian Herman Wiersinga, secularization is characterized by four factors: rationalization (intellectual honesty),

---

9. S. MCFAGUE, *Metaphorical Theology*, London, 1983; ID., *Models of God: Theology for an Ecological Nuclear Age*, London, 1987.

10. D. BONHOEFFER, *Letters and Papers from Prison* (Thoughts for a Baptism), London, 1973, p. 299.

poeticizing (imagery), humanization, functionalization. Hence, the metaphors used in religious language must be thinkable, imaginable, open to experience and practice[11]. Our models will highlight God's immanence more than God's transcendence.

These conditions are very well met in Paul Tillich's metaphors "depth" and "ground of being" as "ultimate concern". In his well-known sermon *Depth*, he says: "The name of this infinite and inexhaustible depth and ground is what the word *God* means. And if that word has not much meaning for you, translate it, and speak of the depths of your life, of the source of your being, of your ultimate concern, of what you take seriously without any reservation"[12].

The American theologian John F. Haught paraphrased Tillich's sermon in *What Is God?* He propounds four models as variants for "depth": future, freedom, beauty, truth. He writes: "I suggest five ways of thinking realistically about God. I shall propose that *God* need not be mistaken as referring to anything alien to the deepest aspects of our common human experience. And I shall argue that the referent of this name is what *all* of us have already experienced to one degree or another, and what we all long to experience even more intimately at the most fundamental levels of our being"[13].

Among Haught's variant models, I consider that of beauty the most revealing for our time. "Our quest for beauty is a quest for the divine. That ultimately satisfying beauty for which we long but which continues to elude us is what the word *God* means. And if that word has not much meaning for you, translate it and speak of the ultimately beautiful for which you are continually searching in the depths of your desire. Perhaps in order to do this you must forget much that you have learned about God, perhaps even that name itself. For if you know that God means ultimate *beauty*, you already know much about the divine. You cannot then call yourself an atheist"[14].

God is not only the *Prima Veritas* (First Truth) and the *Summum Bonum* (Highest Good), but also the Ultimate Beauty. In actual fact, that last model is not at all that new either. We find it already in Augustine[15]. But precisely in our time it stands a fair chance, because postmodernists prefer the paradigm of beauty to that of power.

"Beauty as image of God" means, of course, "*ultimate* beauty". Just like every other imagery, this metaphorical speech must be understood analogically. Here, too, the scholastic method of the three ways is appropriate: the positive, the negative, and the eminent. Also as Beauty, God

11. H. WIERSINGA, *Geloven bij daglicht*, Baarn, 1992, p. 77.

12. P. TILLICH, *The Shaking of the Foundations*, New York, 1962, p. 63.

13. J.F. HAUGHT, *What Is God? How to Think about the Divine*, New York-Mahwah, NJ, 1986, p. 4.

14. *Ibid.*, p. 70.

15. AUGUSTINE, *Confessions* XI,4,6.

is the Wholly Other: we cannot see him "face to face" (1 Cor 13,12). Obviously, the qualifier "ultimate" is important to bring about the 'disclosure'. With this reflection we arrive at the 'linguistic analysis' of the philosophy of language.

A Religious Language

Precisely because, as has been said, God can neither be empirically verified nor rationally demonstrated, God cannot be brought up in a neutral, objectifying manner. Flat propositions such as those used in scientific reports or purely observing coverage are nonsensical here. Their truth can in no way be verified empirically or logically.

Only in subjectivizing speech can the word "God" function meaningfully and thus possibly be true. This subjective language, wherein information is subordinate to dialogue and self-expression, is strongly evocative (symbolic), auto-implicative (subject-centered) and performative (situation-transforming). Meaningful God-talk implies a reference to the 'beyond' of the observable, a self-revelation of the speaking subject and a change of the situation. When I say "God", I obviously refer to a referent outside of me – with "God" I mean more than a concept, a chiffre, a projection –, but still, at the same time, I say something about myself, in such a way that it influences my concrete existence. Something happens to me. The imagery is emotional, personal, embedded in concrete life experiences, and it determines behavior. Strictly speaking, it can not be verified by others, just as little as the meaning and truth of the love song can be checked: "You, you are the salt in my stew, the cream in my coffee, the sugar in my tea"[16].

Of course, God is more than an engaging image; but whether the purely descriptive affirmation "God is" may be meaningful, is not obviously clear. When the statement is a personal expression of, say, faith or hope, then it is functional and hence meaningful. The same seems to apply to the question "Does God exist?", or the cry "God!", or the confession "God:" (with a colon: as a commitment), which are mostly personal and emotional. "God" sounds completely different in the invocation of the pious than in the thought system of the philosopher. The lamentation of the pious psalmist may serve as an example:

Lord, out of the depths I have called to you;
hear my cry, Lord;
let your ears be attentive to my supplication (...)
I wait for the Lord with longing;
I put my hope in his word.
My soul waits for the Lord
more eagerly than watchmen for the morning (Ps 130).

16. W.A. DE PATER, *Taalanalytische perspectieven* (n. 3), p. 25.

Without committing oneself, one cannot say anything meaningful about God. I recall the reply of the German playwright Bertold Brecht to the question, "Whether there is a God?": "Someone asked Mr. N. whether there is a God. Mr. N. said, 'I advise you to reflect upon the outcome of the answer. Would it change your behavior? If it would not change it then we can drop the question. If it would change it, then I can only help you in so far as to say that you have already decided: you need a God"[17].

In the wake of Wittgenstein II, Ian T. Ramsey rightly argued that meaningful speech about God belongs to the "religious language-game". Only there can it function properly. "As in chess, the meaning of a piece is its role in the game. Individual pieces have no meaning outside the whole system of which they are part", writes Wittgenstein in his *Philosophical Investigations*.

It is sufficiently known how the religious language-game operates. Still, let me summarize it briefly. The religious language-game works with models that are derived from our every-day experience and need no further explanation: (God as) life, cause, power, purpose, love, depth, father, mother, friend, goodness, faithfulness, freedom, wisdom, body, light, beauty, etc. The models are adopted and employed in a certain way (qualifier, functor, operator), e.g. various degrees of life, causality, power, purpose, love, depth, fatherhood, motherhood, friendship, etc. God is seen as 'eternal' life, 'first' cause, 'omni'-potence, 'ultimate' purpose, 'endless' love, 'deepest' depth, 'the' father, 'the' mother, 'the' friend. Thus one arrives at the disclosure (the 'Aha-Erlebnis', the 'I see moment': the light dawns, the ice breaks, the penny drops, things come alive)[18]. The disclosure has something surprising and is often enjoyable.

The disclosure is both cognitive and ethical. It is a discernment as well as a commitment. The model adopted makes me see and do something. To say it in the style of Paul Ricoeur: "Le symbole donne à penser *et à faire*". Religious propositions without any personal backing and without any ethical impact are in fact meaningless.

However, the disclosure is not the automatic effect of the qualified models. The 'happening' of the leap over the 'logical gap' between model and disclosure is dependent on three factors: (1) the adaptedness of the models with regard to the reality that must be disclosed (objective resemblance between God and the image: father, mother, friend, depth, power, wisdom, freedom, goodness, beauty); (2) the susceptibility of the addressee with regard to the adopted images (in an agrarian culture: God as shepherd; for feminists: God as mother; for democrats: God as partner; for nature lovers: God as creator; for art lovers: God as beauty); (3) the

17. B. BRECHT, *Kalendergeschichten*, Hamburg, 1953, p. 104.

18. Cf. I.T. RAMSEY, *Religious Language*, London, 1957; ID., *Christian Discourse*, London, 1965; ID., *Freedom and Immortality*, London, 1971.

life context (the same image comes through very differently in a liturgical celebration and in a class community, a club of friends, a political meeting, a sports event).

To Whom Your Heart Adheres

From what is said it became clear that the choice of the models must be made judiciously, taking into account the objective aptitude of the images, the susceptibility of the subject addressed and the concrete *Sitz im Leben* of the God-talk. No image is exclusive and generally valid. Linguistic pluralism is inevitable and indeed enriching. God may have many names and many faces; in fact, he is greater than any name, different from any face. Now God appears as man, then as woman, as father or mother, as friend, white or black, old or young; sometimes as light, fire, water, bread, picturesque landscape, conciliatory gesture; comforting conversation, encouraging smile... All images and symbols.

Only images and symbols? With Tillich one can state: don't say only a symbol, but not less than a symbol[19]. First, we cannot do without images, because God's presence is always 'mediated'[20]. Furthermore, we must interpret, if necessary demythologize, the images. The danger lies only in objectification and monopolization. All images fall short. In this connection, Edward Schillebeeckx speaks of the paradox of the life of faith and mysticism. "Belief in God without conceptions of God is meaningless and even impossible, moreover it is historically ineffective; while on the other hand God's absolute presence shatters all our images and conceptions of God"[21].

God appears in very different shapes, in proportion to the person's life circumstances, personal disposition, actual attitude of mind. A quotation from Niko Kazantzakis's *Zorba the Greek* may explain this[22]: "I closed my eyes, soothed. A quiet, mysterious pleasure took possession of me – as if all that green miracle around me were paradise itself, as if all the freshness, airiness and sober rapture which I was feeling were God. God changes his appearance every second. Blessed is the man who can recognize him in all his disguises. At one moment he is a glass of fresh water, the next your son bouncing on your knees or an enchanting woman, or perhaps merely a morning walk. Little by little, everything around me, without changing shape, became a dream. I was happy. Earth and paradise were one. A flower in the field with a large drop of honey in its

---

19. P. TILLICH, *Dynamics of Faith*, New York, 1958, p. 45.

20. E. SCHILLEBEECKX, *Church: The Human Story of God*, London, 1990, p. 99.

21. *Ibid.*, p. 40.

22. N. KAZANTZAKIS, *Zorba the Greek*, 1959, p. 213 (tr. J.A.T. ROBINSON, *Exploration into God*, London, 1967, p. 151). Cf. H.-E. MERTENS, *Waaraan je hart zich hecht. Geloof als waardenbeleving*, Leuven, [8]1992.

center; that was how life appeared to me. And my soul, a wild bee plundering".

This is a good illustration of the definition of God, given by Martin Luther in his Great Catechism: "To whom your heart adheres and on whom you rely is in fact your God". Everyone has one's god or idol, in the sense of an all dominating, relativizing and radicalizing main value, which is the 'pre-value' of all the other, secondary values. The main value can be everything: money, power, celebrity, sex, race, science, art, friendship, family... When money is the primary value of your whole life, thought and striving, then you always and everywhere follow the advice, "business first", then the name of your idol is dollar, mark or franc. When power and fame are the ideals of your life, so that you see everything else in function of that, your idol has other names, but not those of the Bible. The God of Jesus Christ is called "Love" (1 Jn 4,8).

Two remarks concerning Luther's definition and Kazantzakis's religious experience. When everyone has one's own God (to whom one's heart adheres), don't we end up in an unlimited pluralism and a more than suspect subjectivism? Is the God who is conceived as the main value not purely 'wishful thinking'? Is this not simply a psychological projection without any proper ontological status? Thus we return to our point of departure: *May you imagine everything when you say God?*" – No. But where can we find a valid criterion for truth?

Here again, Christians encounter limits. Their God is not named money, power, celebrity... On the contrary, they opt for another value scale, that of the gospel, which presents as main values, freedom and love for neighbor. What Christians take seriously without any reservation is love for oneself (authenticity) and love for others (solidarity): two dimensions of the one, great Love. Not business first, but love first. "Set your mind on God's kingdom and his justice before everything else, and all the rest will come to you as well" (Mt 6,33). To become oneself through giving oneself to others is the life ideal of Christians. The paradox of the gospel reads thus: "Whoever wants to save his life will lose it, but whoever loses his life for my sake will find it" (Mt 16,26).

God is our 'ultimate concern', "what we take seriously without any reservation". And the reverse as well? – Yes, in the frame of meaning of the evangelical hierarchy of values. "Faith is the state of being ultimately concerned": these are the opening words of Tillich's essay on the *Dynamics of Faith*. Christian faith in God is faith in the 'ultimate concern', which found its perfect and model expression in Jesus of Nazareth. His love is exemplary: "As I have loved you, so you are to love one another" (Jn 13,34). Without explicit reference to the life, message and figure of this Jesus, confessed as the Christ, no authentic 'Christian' faith in God is possible.

Therefore, the Jesus story, which Theo de Boer calls the "little subversive story", has a normative character for the evangelical perception of values and the Christian faith in God[23]. This story leads to the drama at Golgotha and the Easter experiences of the disciples. From a Christian point of view, all conceptions of God are subject to the criticism of the mystery of the Cross and Easter. At Golgotha, the roads of all Christians, to whatever church or confession they may belong, are leading together; but it separates the ways of Christians and non-Christians, theologians and philosophers[24].

Still Many Questions Remain Open

With the reflections on the necessity of a new liberating God-talk, which adopts in a religious language-game metaphors that can be understood, imagined, experienced and practiced, the last word is by far not yet spoken. The metaphors make us think (P. Ricoeur). Theology is more than "a search for models", more than a linguistic-philosophical approach to speech about God, revelation and faith, more than a hermeneutic re-reading of the biblical narrative and other ancient texts. It is not only narrative but discursive as well. As a systematic and scientifically sound reflection on faith experiences from the past and the present, theology cannot do without philosophy. For a long time theology has sought and found inspiration in contemporary philosophical thinking. From prophecy to philosophy was only a step, even a very natural one. Exegesis of the texts asks for further reflection.

The above exposition on language and hermeneutics is, therefore, of a propaedeutic nature: it is only intended as an introduction, be it a most necessary one, to the proper doctrine about God. But this will be dealt with by my colleagues G. De Schrijver, A. Vergote and T. de Boer. Here I am only giving a concise inventory of the present God problem.

Perhaps – I speak very hypothetically – today's number one question is whether God is a person or an impersonal 'power'. The question is far from being merely theoretical. It is "a question that concerns every religious person and certainly every Christian in their deepest being. It concerns one's prayer, faith and hope"[25]. "The theistic image of God has fallen out. But what will replace it? Here, the roads will part"[26]. In New Age circles, preference is given to the impersonal 'divine'. But long before the emergence of New Age, Tillich already criticized supernaturalistic theism. God is not "a being", but "being itself", the most real

---

23. T. DE BOER, *De God van de filosofen en de God van Pascal. Op het grensgebied van filosofie en theologie*, 's-Gravenhage, [2]1991, p. 153.

24. See Paul's message of the Cross in 1 Cor 1,18-25. Cf. J. MOLTMANN, *The Crucified God: The Cross as the Foundation and Criticism of Christian Theology*, London, 1974.

25. P. SCHOONENBERG, *God as Person(al)*, in *Concilium* 105 (1977), p. 80.

26. H.M. VROOM, *Een steen in de vijver*, in ID. (ed.), *De god van de filosofen en de god van de bijbel. Het christelijk godsbeeld in discussie*, Zoetermeer, 1991, p. 10.

and foundational dimension of reality: that was the basic thesis of his plea for a God "beyond the God of theism". God is more than just a person[27].

Obviously, this is closely connected with the relation between transcendence and immanence. It is, in fact, an old problem, and not a question of 'either - or', since it is very clear that God is transcendent in his immanence, and vice versa. Under the influence of the ecology problems, J. Moltmann, D. Sölle and others prefer to highlight God's immanence in their ecological theology of creation[28].

The relationship between creator and creation is in need of continuous reconsideration through the contribution of the natural sciences. "Theology for a Scientific Age": that is the new program[29]. The renewed reflection on the relation between creator and creation ends unavoidably in questions concerning God's changeability and passibility. This problem already received full attention in process thought (A.N. Whitehead, C. Hartshorne, J.B. Cobb) and in Moltmann's theology of the cross. God as becoming. God as crucified. This is very much against the grain of classical theistic conceptions. The debate has started again. But, according to Marcel Sarot, it is actually not a debate "between those who hold that God is immutable *simpliciter* (in all respects) and those who hold that God is mutable *simpliciter* (in all respects), but between those who hold that God is immutable *simpliciter* and those who hold that he is immutable in some respects and mutable in other respects"[30].

Changeability, passibility and becoming "in some respects" alludes, of course, to corporeality as well. According to Luco J. van den Brom, in this case it concerns a "corporeality whose nature must be understood in the higher dimensional system"[31].

This was a lining up of some topical questions. Difficult questions. The answers are far from being self-evident. What is important is that they give a new elan and a new dimension to the faith in the living God of Jesus Christ. Ultimately, that is all that matters.

Willem Geetsstraat 12   Herman-Emiel MERTENS
B-2800 Mechelen

27. P. TILLICH, *The Courage to Be*, New York, 1955.

28. Cf. D. SÖLLE, *To Work and to Love: A Theology of Creation*, Philadelphia, 1984; J. MOLTMANN, *God in Creation*, London, 1985.

29. Cf. A. PEACOCKE, *Theology for a Scientific Age: Being and Becoming – Natural and Divine*, Oxford, 1990.

30. M. SAROT, *God, Passibility and Corporeality*, Kampen, 1992, p. 51.

31. L.J. VAN DEN BROM, *Zou God lichamelijk zijn?*, in *Nederlands Theologisch Tijdschrift* 36 (1982), p. 309. See also his masterful dissertation, *God alomtegenwoordig. God omnipresent*, Kampen, 1982.

CHANGES IN THE UNDERSTANDING
OF THE ATTRIBUTES OF GOD
IN DEISM, NEWTON, AND SPINOZA

THE INFLUENCE OF COSMOLOGICAL REFLECTION
ON RELIGIOUS THOUGHT

1. Introduction

This paper has a limited scope. It sets itself the goal to grapple, in
sordino, with the famous contrast experience Pascal evoked in opposing
the God of Abraham, Isaac, and Jacob (and Jesus) to the God of the
philosophers. It is going to pursue this goal not in a direct, straightforward way, but only indirectly. A straightforward treatment would consist
in picturing at length the way in which inspired authors of the biblical
tradition have named God – the righteous one, the glorious one, the
dependable one, the God of love, fidelity, and mercy – and to contrast
this nomenclature with the attributes of God elaborated in the philosophical tradition – God as first cause, and absolute, omniscient, omnipresent,
and infinite Being. True, this comparative approach has the advantage
of bringing out clearly what is the originality of the biblical revelation,
yet for our purpose, this technique will not be used for the simple reason
that we are going to discuss the impact of cosmological reflection on
religious thought (and vice versa). In this way, cosmological reflection
will be considered in its own right, and only in a subsequent step should
one ask the question as to the extent cosmology sets the parameters
within which the biblical belief in God is going to be rethought, and it
is hoped, *revitalized*. This angle of incidence precludes any first-hand
analysis of the usage of the biblical attributes, but it leaves plenty of
room for an examination of the manner a particular cosmologist tried –
or even omitted – to couch one's biblical belief in the idiom of the philosophy of nature. In the period we are going to examine, the 17th century,
it was still quite common to jump from questions of natural philosophy
to metaphysics. The post-Copernican relocation of humanity's place in
the solar system challenged people to grapple with the similarly relocated
question of God's privileged position in the universe.

Metaphysical reflection possesses its own tradition, which is marked
by historical fluctuations. New attributes or names of God get established,
whereas others pass away. Changes occur in the order of the categoriza-
tion of the names. In contemporary theology, "God, the fellow sufferer
who understands" tends to supersede the Greek conception of an impas-
sive God just as on the social level the God "liberator" tends to topple
the juridical God cherished by hierarchically structured communities. A

comparable overturning of the attributes of God can be discerned in 17th-century metaphysics, and there too, new attributes did not come out of the blue. Just as unprecedented tensions in society create the need for innovating and complementing the attributes of God, so too do unequaled discoveries in science. The dramatic rise of modern science beginning the 17th century projected into the divine intellect the craftsmanship of the engineer (Leibniz), and caused metaphysical reflection to grapple with the spatialization and the naturalization of God (Newton and Spinoza), and with the emancipation of the material world from God (Descartes).

The names we are giving to God can dialectically tell us something about our own ultimate concerns in the human community. This is no surprise if one accepts that the *analogia attributionis* is a solemn naming carried out by human beings who, like us, are concerned about health, bliss, and righteousness. In this light, we name God the supremely strong, blissful, and righteous one, and we realize that, in doing so, we have to discard from this naming the elements that are too much qualified by our own human imperfections such as paternalism, sensationalism, and self-righteousness, to mention just a few examples of inferior qualities that erode the excellence of the divine properties. What we attribute to God and what really "is" in God especially in consideration of God being the cause of all created things is, as Aquinas spells out, never univocally the same because of the inevitable barrier of the "analogy of being"[1]. There-fore, we are ennobled and aided yet also judged and faulted by the names we are attributing to God – and one may add, judged also by the names we are relegating to the background when introducing new ones. This remark applies to the same degree to the naming that arises from the social and historical contexts as to that arising from cosmology and the development of science. There is no neutral usage of the names.

2. Deism: The Divine Intellect and the Clockwork of the World

Keeping to a chronological order, we should normally start with Descartes, for it is upon his achievement that all the authors we are going to treat have developed further. On the other hand, to get from the outset a clear idea of what is deism, there is no system that seems to be more representative than that of Leibniz with whom we shall begin.

1. Leibniz on the Divine Intellect: God as the Architect of the Universe

In Leibniz's doctrine of God, he discussed the question as regards the manner in which God's volition relates to the divine intellect, and likewi-se, of the relationship of divine omnipotence to omniscience. This ques-

---

1. "Impossibile est igitur aliquod de Deo et rebus aliis univoce dici", from AQUINAS, *Summa contra gentiles. I, cp. XXXII*, editio leonina manualis, Roma, 1934, p. 33.

tion was raised in the topic of the creation of the world: does God set out to conceive and create the entities of the world by virtue of an omnipotent decision, or should one not say that this decision must be tempered by God's calculating intellect? The answer to the question is suggested already in the formulation itself. For him, in the order of hierarchy, God's volition must be subordinated to his knowledge. In the *Discours de métaphysique*, he says: "To me it sounds rather strange...that view of Descartes which states that the eternal essences (of things) must be regarded as the effect of God's volition. As I see it, the eternal essences can but be the effect of God's understanding, which as such is not subordinated to the divine will, just as the divine essence does not depend on the divine will". And in a conversation with Dobrensky, January 1695, we read: "The essences are independent of God's volition, they only depend on the divine intellect from which they spring"[2].

What Leibniz wanted to exclude was the government of an arbitrary God, who could decide to lead the course of events sometimes this way and other times that way. God cannot act in a capricious, despotic, or emotionally inconsistent way, for such a behaviour will invalidate God's universal love. A capricious God is the source of division and hatred, whereas a temperate God promotes the maximum harmony that can come out of the coexistence of a variety of human beings and material conditioning factors. Thus, Leibniz attached great importance to God's intelligence, the attribute that is going to ennoble and to judge him. His option for omniscience was inspired by a religious respect that sought to save God's honor, for he deemed that it is only in showing (and conjecturing) the ability of God's intellect to make the relatively small imperfections aid the breakthrough of a greater good, that the Creator can be exempted from an accusation of being a malignant God. True, the world, which God created, undeniably contains dispersed portions of suffering, but these can never in their sum total outweigh the sum total of the good, whether in a person's life or within the progression of history as such.

Leibniz is peeping, so to speak, into the cards of God before the act of creation. At any rate, he boldly reconstructed the basic rules of the game God had to observe while creating the best of the possible worlds. In the realm of thought, where God conceives of the ideas or essences of things, logic sets limits to God's creative fantasy. God can produce mentally only those things that are not contradictory in themselves. This restriction is important, for according to Leibniz's philosophy, ideas that are not contradictory can lay claim to being actually created. Therefore, and this is the second step, God must certainly have good reasons for not letting them immediately rush into existence — the principle of sufficient reason. Here, God's wisdom and prudence must see to it that those

---

2. R. DESCARTES, *Discours de métaphysique*, no 2; R. DESCARTES, *Dialogue with Dobrensky*, quoted in G. GRUA, *Jurisprudence universelle et théodicée selon Leibniz*, Paris, 1953, pp. 272-273.

entities that would be allowed to pass into intra-mundane existence would only be those "ideal" ones, whose existence would be compatible with, or at least, not detrimental to the lattice of the actually existing relations into which they are going to be inserted. A particular essence's claim on existence must be justified from, and harmonious with, the prevailing series of events, whose concatenations tend towards the best. As far as this delicate procedure is concerned, God's wisdom cannot make any mistake since the maker of the pre-established harmony possesses the mighty instrument of the infinitesimal calculus, which allows God to determine which series of events is perfectly compatible ("compossible") with other series of events.

Gaston Grua summarizes this as follows: "1. God, the cause of the existence of all things and the Ground in virtue of which the possibles strain after existence, makes that all the possibles lay claim to existence. For there is no reason why some should lay claim to existence, and others not; 2. So all the possibles compete with each other for having access to existence... 3. The latter (case of all coming into existence) however is impossible, since only some of the possibles turn out to be congruous with others, both in the present and in the future. 4. Providence, thus, decrees that only those series of possibles get access to existence which are going to result in the best of the possible worlds. 5. Thus the best of all the possible worlds is a fact"[3].

This brief sketch of Leibniz's pre-established harmony allows us to discern some salient features of deism. God is presented as the irreproachable architect of the universe, who has laid the foundation of a harmonious universe in which all the cogs interact to make the machine of the world run smoothly. This perfect vision applies to the realm of nature – the cosmos – in the same degree as to the realm of human history. Belief in God the Creator of heaven and earth amounts to recognizing the power of a superior intellect that, from the outset, mapped out a self-sufficient world clock, which the Creator is no longer obliged "to clean now and then by an extraordinary concourse" or "to mend as a clockmaker mends its work"[4]. In the best of the possible worlds, God from all eternity has eliminated already in advance the elements and occurrences that might obstruct the optimal unfolding of the whole.

How should Leibniz be regarded? Some exalt him as a penetrating, mystical soul living in intimate union with God, the monad of the monads. Others blame him for his elitist style. Indeed, his perfectly regulated world can produce a certain type of amicable, well-intentioned people who – in imitation of their God – will tend to eliminate persons and groups who in their opinion have no place in the best of the present

---

3. G. GRUA, *o.c.*, p. 322.
4. A. KOYRÉ, *From the Closed World to the Infinite Universe* (1957), Baltimore-London, 1970, p. 236.

societies. Social justice is not a high priority of the élites in the Leibnizian world system, nor is it a priority of the God who justifies them. Elsewhere I have sketched the line that connects Hegel with Leibniz, and listed the critiques levelled against Hegel from the standpoint of the victims of history[5].

2. Descartes and the Split between Mind and Matter: The Emancipation of Matter from God.

Whereas Leibniz, through his theory of the monads (which are spiritual contractions of matter), overcame the dualism of mind and matter, Descartes, his predecessor, certainly did not. Now, one has to be careful not to confuse this dualism with the old, Platonic dualism, for what caused the Cartesian dualism to come into existence was not the human (quasi-gnostic) fall into matter but the specific internal organization of two domains that, ever since modernity, have become difficult to unite. In the world of science, the human beings have to face up to the mechanistic laws of nature, whereas in their interiority, they experience spiritual freedom, which links them to God. God is believed, at best, to guarantee the co-ordination of these two domains, though there practically is an effective split between the human domain of interiority (res cogitans) and the outer realm of matter and space (res extensa).

From this double-edged perspective, Descartes laid the foundations for a mechanistic conception of the world. The material world is characterized by extension. More in particular, matter is coextensive with space; this means that the whole of space is filled with particles of matter, which are by definition, inert stuff pruned of conscious action. They, however, are capable of interacting with one another and of changing their places in the universe in accordance to the mechanical laws of motion. The particles persevere in their state either of rest or of uniform, straight line motion (cf. Galileo) unless they are compelled to change this state under the impact of mutual collisions: "all the phenomena of nature are produced by particles of matter in motion"[6]. Thus, Descartes could dispense with cosmic intelligences like Aristotle's 55 auxiliary unmoved movers or other esoteric powers in nature. For him, there was only one intelligent unmoved mover (God), who created a self-sustaining world whose elements comply with the laws of motion.

Descartes' theory of motion is best understood when it is read in the context of nascent deism. "In the 17th century, everyone agreed that the origin of motion lay with God. In the beginning, He created matter and

5. See G. DE SCHRIJVER, From Theodicy to Anthropodicy. The Contemporary Acceptance of Nietzsche and the Problem of Suffering, in J. LAMBRECHT (ed.), God and Human Suffering (Louvain Theological and Pastoral Monographies, 3), Louvain, 95-120.

6. R. WESTFALL, The Construction of Modern Science. Mechanisms and Mechanics, Cambridge, (1971), 1977, p. 33.

set it in motion". And once set in motion, matter obeys the principle of inertia: "Nothing is required to *keep* matter in motion: motion is a state, and like every other state, in which matter finds itself, it will continue as long as nothing external operates to change it"[7]. This law practically flows from God's divine immobility, which so to speak, is reflected in the primordial state of inertia which the material things adopt once they have been called into existence by the Creator. On the other hand, it pertains to the world's difference from God that the material particles in it also can have their inertial state changed in conformity with the "law of change" (Descartes' second law). This law says that motion can be transferred – added to one body through substraction from another body – but always in such a way that the total quantity of motion is conserved. "In impact, motion can be transferred from one body to another, but motion itself remains indestructible"[8]; its total quantity cannot grow or diminish, and this conservation of energy is one of the clear indications of the existence of divine providence. "The supreme law of the world is the law of constancy, of conservation. What God has created, he maintains in being". But then comes the following conclusion: "we do not need to inquire about the first cause of the motion of things, *primum movens* and *immobile*; we can simply admit that things started to move at the same time the world was created; and, this being so, it follows therefrom that this motion will never cease, but only pass from subject to subject"[9].

Does this mean that the world has become infinite? By no means. For though God creates a totally self-moving world, this world cannot lay claim to infinity in the strict sense of the word. The only infinite one is God, who just like the human souls (and the angels), has no extension but only spiritual power that, in God's case, is infinite and boundless. In contrast, the extended world can at most be called indefinite or indeterminate since it is impossible to imagine boundaries to it. In a letter addressed to Henry More, Descartes made this clear: "I say therefore that the world is indeterminate or indefinite because I do not recognize in it any limits. But I dare not call it infinite as I perceive that God is greater than the world, not in respect to his extension, because, as I have already said, I do not acknowledge in God any proper extension, but in respect to his perfection"[10]. "Infinity has always been an essential characteristic, or attribute of God, and means the infinite superabundance of his essence, which enables him to 'be his own cause' (causa sui), and to give himself his own existence, which implies necessary existence, a quality which the indefinite or indeterminate self-moving world lacks"[11].

7. *Ibidem*, p. 34.
8. *Ibidem*, p. 33.
9. A. KOYRÉ, *Newtonian Studies*, London, 1965, p. 71.
10. A. KOYRÉ, *From the Closed World* (n. 4), p. 122.
11. *Ibidem*.

Koyré, who we are following here, concludes: "Now Descartes' God is perhaps not the Christian God, but a philosophical one. He is, nevertheless God, not the soul of the world that penetrates, vivifies, and moves it". We can subscribe to this assessment but not without pointing out that it creates new problems, for in materializing space, and in spatializing matter, Descartes emancipated, so to speak, a considerable domain from God's dominion. The spiritual God in the infinite power of Being no longer intervenes as regards the world of material motion which already has become self-acting. True, God's infinity persists as a spiritual power although in such a way that the new infinity, technically called the indefinite extension of the material world, has been subtracted from it. This subtraction is going to ennoble but also fault Descartes. It "ennobles" because it prepared the emancipation of Western culture from traditional patterns of civilization. It faults him because the world in its materiality now is seen no longer as a book that reveals God. From then on, the book of the world started to refer just to itself, to the reliable structures it contains which have been interlocking increasingly upon themselves only, i.e., within the self-sufficiency of a non-necessary being, to put it antithetically.

3. Isaac Newton: The Divinization of Empty Space and the Spatialization of the Deity

In the general scholium of his *Principia Mathematica*, Newton included a profession of faith in which he tried to bridge the gap between God's infinity and the indefinite extension of the material world. In this profession, Newton was manifestly influenced by his contemporary, the neoplatonic thinker Henry More, who in his discussion with Descartes, stressed the importance of regarding as an attribute of God the absolute mathematical space within which all material things are contained. To this "theologoumenon" Newton added his own Old Testament conviction that God is essentially an omnipotent God, who imposes dominion on the whole creation, on human history, and on the natural world alike. God is actively present in the whole universe, and this presence gives birth to (or "constitutes") the co-ordinates of space and time within which all bodies in the universe, the celestial bodies included, perform their perennially ordered motions.

1. God as the Universal Ruler

Let us read now fragments of this profession of faith, and then comment on them after: "This most beautiful system of the sun, planets, and comets, could only proceed from the counsel and dominion of an intelligent and powerful Being. And if the fixed stars are the centers of other like systems, these, being formed by the like wise counsel, must be all subject to the dominion of One; especially since the light of the fixed stars is of the same nature with the light of the sun, and from every system light passes into all the other systems; and lest the systems of the fixed stars should, by their gravity, fall on each other, he hath placed those systems at immense distances the one from one another. This Being governs all things, not as the soul of the world, but as Lord over all; and on account of his dominion he is wont to be called *Lord God*, *pantokratoor*, or *Universal Ruler*; for *God* is a relative word, and has a reference to servants; and *Deity* is the dominion of God not over his own body, as imagined by those who fancy God to be the soul of the world, but over servants. The supreme God is a Being eternal, infinite, absolutely perfect; but a being, however perfect, without dominion, cannot be said to be Lord God...It is the dominion of a spiritual being which constitutes a God; a true, supreme, or imaginary dominion makes a true, supreme, or imaginary God. And from his true dominion it follows that the true God is a living, powerful, and intelligent Being; and, from his other perfections, that he is supreme, or most perfect. He is eternal and infinite, omnipotent and omniscient; that is, his duration reaches from eternity to eternity; his presence from infinity to infinity; he governs all things, and knows all things that are or can be done. He is not eternity and infinity; but eternal and infinite; *he is not duration and space, but he endures and is present. He endures for ever, and is everywhere present; and by existing always, and everywhere constitutes duration and space*"[12].

What is the major difference with Descartes? Certainly not the point that God is not the soul of the universe. Or should it already constitute a difference considering that, in Descartes' view, God as providence hardly has a tie with matter and extension? Newton, on the contrary, linked God not with matter but with empty space, in which a limited quantity of material particles perform their motions. Descartes' God is removed from the material universe; Newton's God is omnipresent in it through the medium of absolute space and absolute time, the unchangeable co-ordinates of all cosmic motions. This implies that Newton's God is much more immanent in the world than Descartes' — immanent, at least, in the spatial and temporal co-ordinates of the universe. God's omnipresence in the medium of space is clearly asserted in the scholium of the *Optics*, where one reads, "What is there in places almost empty of matter, and whence is it that the sun and the planets gravitate towards one another, without dense matter between them? Whence is it that nature does nothing in vain, and whence arises all that order and beauty that we see in the world? To what end are comets, and whence is it that planets move all one and the same way in orbs eccentric while comets move all manner of ways in orbs very eccentric, and what hinders the

---

12. I. NEWTON, *Principia Mathematica* (1686): I *The Motion of Bodies*, II *The System of the World*, ed. Cajori, Berkeley-Los Angeles, 1966, p. 545 (italics mine).

fixed stars from falling upon one another? How come the bodies of animals were contrived with so much art, and for what ends were their several parts? Was the eye contrived without skill in optics and the ear without knowledge of sounds?...And these things being rightly dispatched, does it not appear from phenomena that there is a Being, incorporeal, living, intelligent, omnipresent, *who in infinite space, as it were in his sensory organ, sees the things themselves intimately,* and thoroughly perceives them, and comprehends them wholly by their immediate presence to himself"[13]?

To bring out the difference between Descartes' and Newton's universe, nobody is more eloquent than Voltaire. "A Frenchman who arrives in London", says Voltaire, "finds himself in a totally changed world. He left the world *full*; he finds it *empty*. In Paris the universe is composed of vortices of subtle matter; in London there is nothing of that kind. In Paris everything is explained by pressure which nobody understands; in London by attraction which nobody understands either". Indeed, the Newtonian world is chiefly composed of void, and it is in this void, as Koyré points out, that the force of gravity, which attracts bodies to each other, carries out its unifying task. Space "is an infinite void, and only a very small part of it is filled up, or occupied, by matter, by bodies which, indifferent, and unattached, move freely and perfectly unhampered in — and through — that boundless and bottomless abyss. And yet it is a world and not a chaotic congeries of isolated and mutually alien particles. This, because all of these are bound together by a very simple mathematical law of connection and integration — the law of attraction — according to which *every one of them is related to and united with every other.* Thus each one takes its part and plays its role in the building of the *systema mundi*"[14].

The dance of the material particles in the void is kept within limits by the co-ordinates of absolute time and absolute space, which Newton introduced for mathematical and religious reasons. Mathematically speaking, Newton had to ascertain, first, that space, in its immensity, is an independent receptacle within which the particles of matter — and the conglomerates of mass points such as the stars and the planets — perform their well-regulated motions and accelerations; second, that only if the spatial container itself is never subject to change in the course of time, can the various changes in the universe get organized purposefully. Both assertions agree with the basic principles of Euclidean geometry, which was the only one known in those days. Only the objective realities of absolute, unchangeable space and of absolute, unchangeable time can

---

13. I. NEWTON, *Optics, or a Treatise of the Reflections, Refractions, Inflections, and Volours of Light* (1704), London, 1730, p. 356 (italics mine).
14. A. KOYRÉ, *Newtonian Studies* (n. 9), p. 14.

"guarantee the validity of the mathematical constructions of physics"[15]. Were these realities not absolutely reliable, independent, and unchangeable, one would have no certainty at all concerning the correct functioning of mathematical procedures in physics; time and space must be absolute values if the laws of nature are to work without exception. Besides this, however, Newton had also his religious reasons for maintaining the objective realities of absolute space and time since, for him, they constituted the sensory organ of God for perceiving things and assigning them their place in the universe.

It is worth noting that absolute space and time were defined in parallel to the classical definition of the world's relation to God, to a God who strictly has no real relation to the world. "Absolute space, in its own nature without relation to anything external, remains always similar and immovable", and "absolute, true, and mathematical time, of itself, and from its own nature, flows equably without relation to anything external, and by another term is called duration"[16]. Absolute time endures from eternity to eternity, whereas we, from our changing place in the universe, are only able to grasp this absolute duration by channelling it to our sensory and comparative estimation of sequences of time. This we do, for example, whenever we infer the demarcation of months and years from the changing astronomical positions of stars and planets. Absolute space too, which is immovable from infinity to infinity, can be grasped by us only by relating it to something changing, though in itself it is unchangeable.

In short, for Newton, all the motions in the universe relate to – and are contained within – absolute space and time, whereas this pair has no relation whatsoever to the motions. From this, it follows that absolute space and time are not in the least influenced by the various motions in the universe of which they constitute the unchangeable co-ordinates. The absolute co-ordinates make the various kinds of ordered motion conceivable and possible, and *not vice versa*. This calls to mind the classical definition of Aquinas: God does not relate to the universe, whereas all the things in it inevitably relate to God from whom they "borrow" their existence, whatever this qualified existence might be[17]. Now, it is this religious truth that Newton wanted to intimate through a reflection on true mathematical time and space. For him, an analogy existed between God's eternity, infinity, and immutability on the one hand, and the eternity, infinity, and immutability of absolute space and time on the other. But how exactly did he understand this analogy?

15. J. MERLEAU-PONTY and B. MORANDO, *Les trois étappes de la cosmologie*, Paris, 1971, p. 94.

16. I. NEWTON, *Principia Mathematica* (n. 12), p. 7.

17. Cf. AQUINAS, *Summa Theologiae. I, q. 13, art. 7*, ed. Marietti, Torino-Roma, 1950, p. 70: "creaturae realiter referunter ad ipsum Deum; sed in Deo non est aliqua realis relatio eius ad creaturas, sed secundum rationem tantum, inquantum creaturae referuntur ad ipsum".

2. Absolute Space as God's sensorium

In classical theology, boundless time and space (eternity and immensity) have been associated with God's might. They functioned as attributes of God only in so far as they denoted a time and space that were clearly distinct from created time and space. The denotations immensity (*immensitas*), infinity, and eternity (*aeternitas*) were used to highlight the divine sovereignty, which endures for ever and ever – *per omnia saecula saeculorum* – and which is not in the least menaced by the vicissitudes of finite existence (*immobilitas Dei*). Compared with God, the eternal one, all the metaphors describing the cosmos' vastness and the durability of the heavens consequently are bound to be resolved into nought. In Newton's days, however, the notions immensity, infinity, and eternity began to be used also in mathematics to designate the absolute and independent co-ordinates to which all the spatial and temporal motions in the universe related. Absolute space was understood as remaining always independent, identical, and immovable, and absolute time as always flowing equably and enduring in this independent state from infinity to infinity. From this development, the temporal and spatial attributes of God, and practically, the deity itself were dislodged from their supra-celestial position, and absorbed into the cosmic realm. The attributes got inserted into a domain that, from the perspective of classical theology, was God's creature, created out of nothing.

Facing up to this awkward situation, Henry More (1614-1684), a well-known Christian neoplatonist in Cambridge who died a few years before the publication of Newton's *Principia Mathematica*, tried to harmonize the mathematical concepts of absolute space and time with God's infinity. For him, absolute space is "eternal and therefore uncreated. But the (material) things that are in space by no means participate in these properties. Quite the contrary; they are temporal and mutable and are created by God in the eternal space and at a certain moment of the eternal time"[18]. In an anti-Cartesian mood, More separated space from matter; he set free the infinite void of space so much so that, as Koyré says, he raised "it to the dignity of an attribute of God, and of an organ in which and through which God creates and maintains His World, a finite world, limited in space as well as in time, as an infinite creature is an utterly contradictory concept"[19]. In other words, for More, the universe, taken in its material components, is essentially finite, created, and contained within absolute space, which as such is uncreated, infinite, and sharing in the Creator's attributes of integrity, indivisibility, eternity, and immobility. Moreover, this "divine" space was seen as constituting the organ in which and through which God's creative might pours into the material world. Absolute space and absolute time, thus, waver between being a

18. A. KOYRÉ, *From the Closed World* (n. 4), p. 150.
19. *Ibidem*, p. 153.

strict attribute of God and a co-eternal organ the deity uses to create and
sustain the universe. Now, this oscillation raises the question as to which
of the two agents do infinity and necessary existence pertain: to the sole
God Creator or to this God Creator plus the Godhead's two co-eternal
cosmic hands, absolute space and time, through which God intervenes
in the universe? From another perspective, these divine organs are also
the mathematical co-ordinates *of* the universe, and thus, *part* of the
universe in spite of their independence from the motions that take place
in it. Is infinity God's sole prerogative or is it also an attribute of the
universe's spatial and temporal co-ordinates? More did not back away
from "the conclusions of his premises with which he announced to the
world the spatiality of God and the divinity of space"[20].

This oscillation in the attribution of infinity and eternity can be found
also in Newton. In the passages where he adopts an Old Testament style,
he emphatically declares that infinity, eternity, and omnipresence are the
personal characteristics of the deity ("He is not eternity and infinity; but
eternal and infinite; he is not duration and space, but he endures and is
present. He endures for ever, and is everywhere present"). Yet elsewhere,
in the wake of More's neoplatonism, he attributes infinity and perma-
nence also to the universe's absolute space and time in so far as they
comprise the *sensorium* God uses to act upon creation. He, however, then
tried to harmonize both statements by explaining how the absolute mathematical space and time "flow" from and are subordinated to God's absolute Being. It is "by existing always, and everywhere", he says, that God
"*constitutes* duration and space", i.e., that God calls duration and space
into existence as the sensory organ the Deity uses for perceiving cosmic
reality. This way, the Old Testament deity was both affirmed and mitigated; mitigated because it was tacitly acknowledged that absolute time and
space are emanations from the deity before the creation of matter. The
aspect of emanation was not at all shocking to the neoplatonist More or
to Samuel Clark, Newton's theological adviser, who in his correspondence with Leibniz wrote: "that God exists in all the spaces and in all
the times, these words mean only that he is omnipresent and eternal, that
is that boundless space and time are *necessary consequences* of his
existence and not that space and time are beings distinct from him, and
in which he exists"[21].

Absolute time and space are on the side of God, the immaterial Being
par excellence. This includes the immaterial force of gravity, which God
uses as a "second cause" in creation to order the world, to assign their
place to every thing, and to retain the planets on their orbs. The planets
are revolving in free space ruled only by the force of gravity, which
operates according to the quantity of solid matter the interacting bodies

20. *Ibidem*, p. 152.
21. *Ibidem*, p. 271.

contain, which propagates its power on all sides towards immense distances, and which decreases always as the inverse square of the distances. Now, this force of gravity, which apparently arises from the celestial bodies, is in Newton's eyes neither material nor an innate property of the bodies. It is rather a force that shares in God's concealment and might, but its constant effects can be tested empirically. In this quality, it reveals the workings of the deity. Wherever this force is visibly at work, like in the steady revolutions of the planets, one can discern the presence of the Creator, who in activating this force, lets the divine face shine on the universe from above the co-ordinates of absolute space and time.

Conclusion. We have seen that Descartes subtracted the indefinite extension of the material world from God's infinity. In the case of Newton, however, we are not dealing with a subtraction but an addition. The mathematical co-ordinates of absolute time and space were added to God's personal infinity. This way, space became divinized and God spatialized (i.e., "extended" into the void from which God sustains the world and acts upon it through the mysterious force of gravity). The purpose of this addition is clear. It was done to safeguard the divine omnipotence of the Creator. To what extent is Newton ennobled and judged by this expansion of God's attribute of infinity? It is commendable that he took pains to preserve a place of dominion for God in the void of space; furthermore, he refused to speculate the inner nature of the force of gravity, whose effects, he has shown, are always attaining their goal. This fervour for God ennobles him especially when one contrasts him with the Newtonian school, which after his death, abandoned every metaphysical concern and ended up in sheer positivism. Newtonian science and not Newton's theology would hold sway over the next two and a half centuries. Now with Einstein's theory of relativity, which demonstrates that there are no such things as absolute space and absolute time, Newton's expansion of God's infinity by the addition of space becomes unacceptable. The relation between matter and its spatial and temporal co-ordinates is far more complex than Newton thought it was.

4. Spinoza: Deus sive natura: The Naturalization of God and the Divinization of Nature

Descartes and Leibniz paved the way for deism and its God who does not need to rewind the clock of the world. Newton then sought to restore the might of God in creation, yet from the scientific vantage-point, his followers were no better than the followers of Descartes and Leibniz. The Newtonians admired Newton much more for his scientific achievements than for his religious considerations. Within a few generations, the scientists became interested no longer in the mysterious causes of the working of the laws of physics but only in the mathematical formulae and their palpable results. Scientism absorbed the theological questions, and left God either in the incomprehensible infinitude outside the world in which divinity no longer acted or in the realm of the void, which practically became God's grave. In these developments, religion and religiosity had little chance to survive. Before that, however, in the decades separating the productive years of Descartes from Newton's, Baruch Spinoza in the Netherlands worked out his new religious synthesis of God, mind, and matter.

1. The Divine Substance and Its Attributes

Spinoza's source for his own system was, besides Moses Maimonides, Descartes, though it is doubtful whether or not he attached the same basic meaning to the notion of matter as Descartes did. Spinoza's point of departure is, first, that there is only one substance, the substance of God, which unfolds itself into various modes or expressions; second, that this one substance must be considered both under the aspect or attribute of thought and the attribute of extension. The ontological proof of God's existence makes it clear that God is the sole substance whose definition — ens a se — requires its necessary existence, whereas all other substances unavoidably depend on God's necessary substance. All the entities in the universe are modes, expressions, and presentations of the deity "in which" they live and move and which itself lives and moves "in them". At this level, Spinoza apparently appropriated the scholastic notion of the finite entities' participation in the infinite, a notion that he, however, radicalizes. He holds that the finite entities have their true Being "in God", yet in practice, they live out their lives in a mixture of truth and error, authentic values and unchecked passions, and physical powers and limitations, a mixture that is indicative of their situation as participating entities. Their true Being, nevertheless, comes to the fore in the way in which they endeavour to persevere in their dynamic "act" of Being (conatus essendi). This "endeavour to be" makes them aspire for true knowledge so that they can acknowledge their place in the universe, which in turn, is the grandiose setting in which the necessary existing divine substance makes its multifarious appearances in and through its unfolding modes or expressions.

What Spinoza has said till now is but a variant of mystical panentheism that can be found in Plotinus or Meister Eckhart. He nevertheless moved beyond them by placing this mystical panentheism within the context of 17th-century science. The scientific practice of Galileo, Descartes, and Huygens made it clear to Spinoza that physical reality can be fathomed, that its fundamental laws can be uncovered with accuracy. Nature lays open to the scrutiny of the intellect, which in turn is able to reconstruct nature's fundamental laws. From this it follows that the intellect's logic converges with the logic of nature and vice versa. In a daring way, and so to speak anticipating Hegel, Spinoza posits a convergence if not an identity between our a priori mental constructions and the scientific generalizations inferred from the empirical study of nature. "The hidden assumption of Spinoza's philosophy is that reality and conception *coincide*, so that relations between ideas correspond exactly to relations in reality"[22]. Now, this hidden assumption sheds light on Spinoza's understanding of the attributes of God, and more specifically, on his selection of two of them, thought and extension, as the most salient of God's inexhaustible attributes. "Spinoza identifies two attributes of God: thought and extension. The first is the system of ideas, the second that of physical objects. Our physical science is not a deductive system, but a series of generalizations based on observation of 'finite modes'. Nevertheless, our very procedure, in deriving from there a lawlike description of the 'infinite' modes, presupposes the possibility of a deductive science. Such a science of 'extension' would provide complete knowledge of a self-dependent totality"[23].

This citation requires some explanation. First of all, for Spinoza, the divine substance has necessary existence "in and of itself" because it is "that of which a conception can be formed independently of any other conception"[24]. But then, he goes on to define the notion of "attribute" in a way that is no longer that of classical theism. Indeed, the classical *analogia attributionis* ascribed to God a multiplicity of properties but under the provision that they had to be elevated first to their utmost perfection by cleansing them of all the crude connotations that clash with the purity of the most simple Being. The underlying idea is that the unfathomable fountain-head of creation contains within Itself all the noble properties of the world in a fully pre-eminent fashion and not just in the mode of our univocal naming. The way the Deity "lives out" ("embodies" is too anthropomorphic and cosmomorphic) the properties or attributes always exceeds the power of human understanding. Not so, however, for Spinoza. He is not interested in the "analogy of being" or in the "supra-rational" way of predicating properties to God. His predication rests on the "univocity of being" (to use scholastic language). This means that the exploration of the properties of God is a rational enterprise. Hence, his definition: "by attribute I mean that which the intellect perceives as constituting the essence of substance"[25]. Now, the two basic properties or attributes that the intellect predicates to be constitutive of the divine substance are "God unfolding in the world of thought" and "God unfolding in the world of extension" This again is in tune with the hidden scientific assumption that "the order and connection of ideas is the same as the order and connection of things"[26].

22. R. SCRUTON, *Spinoza*, Oxford, 1986, p. 36.

23. *Ibidem*, p. 45.

24. SPINOZA, *The Ethics (Ethica ordine geometrico demonstrata). I, Definition 3* (1677), ed. S. Charter, Washington, 1981, p. 29.

25. *Ethica*, I, def. 4, p. 20.

26. *Ethica*, II, prop. 7, p. VIII, p. 69.

For Spinoza, the two salient attributes do not divide the divine substance, for "substance thinking and substance extended are one and the same substance", "comprehended now through one attribute, now through the other"[27]. With respect to our knowledge of God, it follows that there are basically two complementary ways to get to know how things — and also how we ourselves — are by causal concatenation comprised in the divine substance from which all the modes of Being (or expressive modifications of the divine substance) derive their logically conceived existence. These two complementary ways are the study of the concatenation of causes in the realm of thought and the study of the concatenation of causes in the realm of physics. "As long as we consider things as modes of thinking, we must explain the whole order of nature; or the whole chain of causes, through the attribute of thought only. And in so far as we consider things as modes of extension, we must explain the whole order of nature through the attribute of extension (and so on, in the case of other attributes)"[28].

It is here that we suddenly see the provocative identification of God and nature. It dawns upon us what the impact of the one divine substance means if we come to realize how the whole order of nature intrinsically relates to the one God/Nature and if we realize this intrinsic bond by delving alternately into the attribute of thought and the attribute of extension. Let us take it for granted that in ethics the exploration of the causal chain primarily takes place in the order of ideas. Even then, the method of ethics will have to teach us something about the unity of bodily and mental existence. Spinoza pleads for a positive reappraisal of the body. In an attempt to bridge the Cartesian dualism, he envisions the human being as a "thinking body". The human mind is rooted entirely in nature from which it draws its most authentic feelings and emotions as well as its potent intuitions and thoughts. To comparatively weigh the worth of emotions, and to discern through causal reasoning what is authentic in them and what is not, prepares us to see ourselves in God and to love the deity. Spinoza says, "He who clearly and distinctly understands himself and his emotions loves God, and so much the more in proportion as he understands himself and his emotions"[29]. The human being ought to learn to feel at home and to find his and her place in the complex world of interacting impulses and forces. Above all, a human has to learn to think and feel in an ordered way on the basis of ever abundant and rich experiences. Step by step, Spinoza set out to show how much we, in our bodily-spiritual existence, can come to see ourselves as parts — and modes — of the divine substance, whose intellect pervades the whole of the material universe. The mystical rose blooms when one succeeds

27. *Ibidem*, corollary, p. 69.
28. *Ibidem*, p. 70.
29. *Ethica*, V, prop. 15, p. 229.

in seeing God as the "indwelling cause of all things"[30], a cause that, for too long, we have deemed to be external to us but which now we begin to perceive as the One Substance that internally lures the things towards their "endeavour to persevere in existing" (*conatus essendi*).

It is clear that Spinoza's reflections on human psychology cannot be dissociated from a science of the physical world. We now turn to this alternate vantage-point from which to look at the world in its totality. Just as the vantage-point – or the attribute – of thought brings us in contact with the eternal substance, so too does the vantage-point of the science of extension. The extended things also are comprised within the eternal substance. Extension is as eternal as "the absolutely infinite being", "which contains in its essence whatever expresses reality, and involves no negation"[31]. From this, it follows that extension is the matrix in which the laws of nature are going to be inscribed. Extension contains all the principles and laws that are going to regulate the behaviour of all the things extended; here, however, one has to make a distinction. All extended things are, to be sure, modes of the one divine substance (for they are modes whose existence cannot be envisaged without envisaging something else upon which their existence depends), yet the material things are just finite modes, whereas the laws of nature, under which the physical behaviour of these things fall, are themselves infinite modes. This distinction is logical, for the singular material things – our own thinking bodies included – are fleeting and replaceable by other material things within the same species or class. Singular material elements, therefore, cannot be durable, though they are contained within the eternal matrix of extension. On the other hand, the *laws* of nature are not in the same degree fleeting and replaceable; they go on enjoining their coercion even if the world gets populated by novel configurations of matter and fresh material entities. Still however, they lack the proper eternity or infinity that extension, as a real attribute of God/Nature, possesses. The laws of nature altogether are not an attribute of the deity; they only "follow" and "flow" from the divine attribute of extension[32]. This implies that the laws of nature, in principle, could have acted in a way different from what they are doing now (i.e., nature could have had a different set of natural laws) *if* this *had been* the ruling of the attribute of extension.

Let's make this consideration on the laws of nature a bit more concrete. Spinoza certainly must have taken cognizance of Descartes' two laws of motion: one saying that bodies in a state of rest or uniform, straight line motion tend to persevere in that state unless they are compelled to change that state under the impact of mutual collisions (the law of iner-

30. *Ethica*, I, prop. 18, p. 45.

31. *Ibidem*, def. VI, and explanation, p. 29.

32. "A mode, therefore, which necessarily exists as infinite, must follow from the absolute nature of some attribute of God"; *ibidem*, prop. 23, proof, p. 48.

tia); the other that motion can be transferred – added to one body through substraction from another body – and that if this happens, the state of inertia turns into that of acceleration. Now, these two laws, along with their basic presuppositions such as the inanimate nature of matter and the principle of the conservation of energy (motion itself is indestructible) are "infinite modes" or appearances of the one thinking and extended substance; they remain in force even when the bodies upon which they act perish and are replaced by other bodies, yet for their durability, they in turn depend on the eternal and necessary character of extension. The unchanging workings of the laws of physics prompt us to acknowledge the unchanging higher condition upon which they depend, i.e., the absolute nature of the attribute of extension (though in principle, the superior cause, which is extension, might have grounded a different kind of physical laws, in accordance with its own essential properties).

Spinoza died in 1677, the year in which his *Ethics* was completed. Ten years later, Newton published his *Principia Mathematica*. If Spinoza had been able to take cognizance of the law of gravity, how would he have probably assessed it from his own vantage-point? He certainly would have explained gravity in a mechanistic way. For him, the law of gravity, which makes bodies fall in space through action at a distance, would have been only a law of physics, which is always acting the same way because of the unchanging coercion flowing from the absolute nature of God's attribute of extension. In no case would he have been willing to accept the void as the place of God's action in the world, for in his system, there is no place for an immaterial God or for a specially interfering providence. Feelings of awe before the personal biblical God, ruler and master of the universe, whose spiritual might retains the planets on their orbs, are alien to the Jew Spinoza. In line with his scientific method – which postulated the comprehensibility of the causal chains of nature – he rather opts for a submission to causal effects, which are inevitable, and if possible, opts for a committed love of one's destiny (*amor fati*) within the universe. In his eyes, the human beings can only exercise their freedom by wholeheartedly acknowledging the serial coercion of things, i.e., their logically necessary causation by God/Nature. Thus, e.g., if a gale blows the tiles off a roof and someone gets hit by the falling pieces, this is no reason for cursing God in heavens, who apparently has nothing to do with this accident. The only appropriate reaction is to put up with the negative side-effects of natural processes, which as one perceives, are beneficial on the whole. There is no reason for letting oneself be carried away by feelings of hatred and anger against "mother nature", which is how this divine substance is sometimes called today.

2. The Three Kinds of Knowledge

This leads us to the difference between Spinoza's three kinds of knowledge. The first kind of knowledge is that of traditional believers who uncritically accept that all the events in the world are pre-ordained by God's providence; the second kind has integrated the findings of the natural sciences and modern cosmology, whereas the third kind initiates us into a mystical love of the universe.

The first kind of knowledge is characterized by a certain *naiveté*; it is found in religious communities that believe in God as a personal being. For them, God is a personal ruler and father who punishes the sinners and redeems those who repent their trespasses. Spinoza rejects this belief in God for several reasons. First of all, he thinks that these pious people actually do not understand the words they are using or the properties they are ascribing to God, for example, God as Father or God as Redeemer. They still dream of a God who is not intrinsically involved in the workings of nature and from whom they expect and to whom they beseech, on their behalf, the miraculous suspension of the serial chain of determinant causes. Second, such a belief is still too anthropocentric; it starts from the assumption that God "has made all things for man", so that "man may worship God" in man-made synagogues and churches[33]. This anthropocentric vision of God, however, blocks the road to a *naturalistic* piety; it tends to read too many man-oriented finalities into the workings of nature and so averts us from loving our earthly destiny in communion with the whole of nature. Third, the belief in a personal God who reigns in heaven, and from there runs his dispensation of grace, has boosted a lot of "prejudices about good and wrong, praise and blame, order and confusion, beauty and ugliness"[34]. Spinoza was horrified by religious intolerance, which originates from sectarian conceptions of the deity. For him, to ascribe a quasi-human personality to God amounts to using God as a sacred canopy to justify the dramatic effects of one's own unchecked passions: self-righteousness and hatred. Each sect pretends to possess a higher truth that the others miss. This stance brought him into conflict with the Jewish community in Amsterdam which excommunicated him.

The second kind of knowledge has integrated scientific knowledge into a *panentheistic* vision of the world. The result is resignation in – and religious acceptance of – one's place in the whole of nature, a place which is inevitably determined by the workings of nature which allow no exception. Spinoza says, "Nothing comes to pass in nature, which can be set down to be a flaw therein; for nature is always the same, and everywhere one and the same in her efficacy and power of action; that is, nature's laws and ordinances, whereby all things come to pass and change from one form to another, are always and everywhere the same, so that there should be one and the same method of understanding the nature of things whatsoever, namely through nature's universal laws and rules"[35]. But besides the insight into the iron cage of necessity, the study

---

33. *Ethica*, I, Appendix, p. 57.
34. *Ibidem*.
35. *Ethica*, III, Introduction, p. 146.

of nature's laws and rules is going to arouse an intense intellectual delight in so far as one begins to understand how all things, through their chains of necessary causation, flow from the eternal substance of God/-Nature. Inescapable destiny, couched in the deterministic unrolling of natural laws, is one aspect of this ruthless discovery. Delight in it, because of the discovery that nothing in the universe and in our lives truly happens at random or just due to casual, unexplained contingencies, is the other side of the coin and a step that invites ecstasy and intensifies the scientists' perseverance in scrutinizing the laws of nature. Spinoza, thus, moved beyond a purely anthropocentric approach to worship. Thanks to the integration of science into mysticism, he reached an objective standpoint, that is, the universe and its manifold unfolding through logically necessary laws. This objective standpoint taught him to take delight in the substantial, ramified causation that dwells in the whole of nature. He says, "Nothing in the universe is contingent, but all things are conditioned to exist and to operate in a particular manner by the necessity of the divine nature"[36].

Then comes the third kind of knowledge, the intuitive "intellectual love" (*amor intellectualis*). This love dawns upon us when we begin to contemplate the very individual things under the "form of eternity", i.e., as possessing an eternal value in spite of their transience. He says, "things are conceived by us in two ways: either as existing in relation to a given time and place, or as contained in God/Nature and following from the necessity of the divine being. Whatever we conceive in this second way as true and real we conceive under the form of eternity, and their ideas involve the eternal and infinite essence of God, as shown in II, XLV and note"[37]. This note referred to says: "I am speaking, I repeat, of the very existence of particular things, in so far as they are 'in' God/Nature. For although each particular thing be conditioned by another particular thing to exist in a given way, yet the force whereby each particular thing perseveres in existing follows from the eternal necessity of God's nature"[38]. In spite of nature's acting in exactly the same way everywhere, there is also the marvel that particular things, in an astonishing variety, are displaying their own unique perseverance in existing. Now, to experience this power of perseverance in existing – in oneself and in the particular entities in the universe, of which one is also part – amounts to looking at the universe "through the eyes of eternity". The vital eternity of the universe discloses itself in a tremendous contrast-effect in and through the beauty of the *conatus essendi* of the varied particular things. This is the "immortal" perseverance, which they possess and display in spite of the anonymous causations that gave birth to them

36. *Ethica*, I, prop. 29, p. VII.
37. *Ethica*, V, prop. 29, note p. 236.
38. *Ethica*, II, prop. XLV, p. 98.

as transient beings. He says, "The more we understand particular things, the more we understand God"[39]. The particular things constitute, in fact, the so many varied "modes by which the attributes of God are expressed in a fixed and definite manner"[40].

How does the third kind of knowledge relate to the second kind of knowledge? And what is their difference? The commentators are divided over this issue. What is certain is that, in both cases, we are dealing with experiences of satisfaction and joy in spite of the overall deterministic climate in which Spinoza's mysticism is rooted. Still, there are differences. In the second kind of knowledge – the realization that all things and events are determined by physical laws – the joy seems to flow from the insight into these laws. This leads, in turn, to a high respect for the objective disposition of things in nature and to an appreciation of how they are both the outcome (*natura naturata*) and the eventful culmination (*natura naturans*) of nature's workings. In other words, the more one knows these laws, the more is one astonished that they can produce so many marvelous things, and the more is one transported to an emotional rapture that accompanies the scientific discovery. This emotional rapture comes to the fore, e.g., when contemporary scientists with an evolutionary perspective, begin to ask themselves the question whether or not the universe has been unfolding itself and making us, human beings endowed with intellect and radically rooted in the materiality of that universe, for the purpose of leading us to an ultimate understanding of the hidden mechanisms of this expansive development (the anthropic principle).

This intellectual rapture apparently prepares one for the next experience, the mystical love of the universe or of God/Nature. This third kind of knowledge is built on various contrast-effects: the clash between the "terrifying side of nature" and its laudatory worth, between one's personal, affective relationship to nature and the latter's rather impersonal face, and between things so eternally beautiful and the anonymous womb of nature, which has brought them forth and into which they are going to disappear. "Strange as it may sound, it seems possible that in relating personally to such a 'God', we are not overpowered by terror, but come to feel joy in the awareness of our immersion in such a 'God', and even come to 'love' 'God or Nature', although it is so unlike a personal being"[41]. The "things eternally beautiful" call to mind Duns Scotus' and Hopkins' reverence for the unique character of things: "All things counter, original, spare, strange". But while these authors derived the unique character of things from the unique beauty of the One – the transcendent immaterial God – of which they were the outflow in materiality, finitude,

---

39. *Ethica*, V, prop. 24, p. 234.

40. *Ethica*, I, prop. 25, note p. 49.

41. H. DE DIJN, *Wisdom and Theoretical Knowledge in Spinoza*, in R. CURLEY and P.-F. MOREAU (ed.), *Spinoza. Issues and Directions. The Proceedings of the Chicago Spinoza Conference*, Leiden-New York, 147-156, p. 152.

and time, Spinoza's appreciation of each thing's uniqueness is based on an analysis of the world in terms of mechanistic causation, which only in a next step and by way of contrast, is crowned by an intuitive "grasp of things according to their particular essences as they immanently issue from God (God/Nature)"[42].

In terms of their mechanistic causation, the particular things are the outcome of a network of physical causes. They ought to be analysed as such in order to do away with the illusion that they are something special or miraculous in a world that, for the rest, is governed by brute physical laws. Having acquired this scientific knowledge of things and ourselves, it may happen, in a flash of insight, that at once one grasps the emergence of the particular things as grounded in the *inner* design of God/Nature, an emergence understood now as immanent, logical unfolding, and not as the pure working of external, mechanical causes. This complementary view does not annul the awareness of the impact of external causes on the formation of particular entities, but rather allows us to perceive the same process of construction "from within", from the vantage-point of these entities' logical and ontological place "in" the one substance from which all things issue forth internally through an immanent emanation. "God/Nature is the indwelling and not the transient cause of all things"[43]. The particular things in the universe, including our own particular modes of existence, are assessed and mystically loved as the unforgettable unfolding of the one divine substance into the splendid multiplicity of very particular faces. Placed in this process of unfolding, the so many unique faces acquire a coating of eternity in the midst of finitude, whereas the formerly anonymous womb of nature discloses itself now as the one creative power of the universe, a power palpable in the perseverance in existence manifested by all things.

Applied to the understanding of one's own personality, Spinoza's third kind of knowledge attempts to dislodge the Ego from one's naive and often egoistic self-image by inviting the person to scientifically look at all the objective factors that have been formative of one's life story, factors such as the causal processes of genetics and neurophysiology which have been "blindly" at work. This leads to the frightening knowledge of one's inescapable genetic code and hereditary material. Other factors are social, political, and psychological; these lead to the discovery of one's historical determinisms. Having gone through this painful "dark enlightenment", the person is then asked to re-examine oneself in this light *and* "under the aspect of eternity". Under the latter aspect, it may occur that one suddenly recognizes that this person, whose destiny is totally conditioned by external factors, has *also* been "willed" as a unique

---

42. Y. YOVEL, *The Third Kind of Knowledge as Alternative Salvation*, in R. CURLEY and P.-F. MOREAU (ed.), *Spinoza* (n. 41), 157-175, p. 168.

43. *Ethica*, I, prop. 18, p. VI.

human being through the "immanent causation" of the one substantial ground of God/Nature, which graciously unfolds itself into the many faces of particular existence. We are "in" the cosmos, embraced by it, and the cosmos is "in" us, *particularized* in us! This emotional holistic experience makes one weep for joy because of the type of person one "is" and "has become" within the whole of the universe: a person endowed with a particular perseverance in existence and capable of enjoying authentic feelings. This joy is the moment of eternity in the midst of finitude. In that ecstatic moment, the person feels oneself as eternal as the ecstatic core of the universe. All this in spite of the realization that the divine substance is not only eternal but also sempiternal, for only the duration of God/Nature is without temporal limits, whereas all its transient particular manifestations are bound to die and to return into the womb that brought them forth.

To conclude this analysis of Spinoza, it is appropriate to ask two questions: first, what has he done with the attributes of God?; second, how is his revision of the attributes going to ennoble and to judge him? Well, it is clear that Spinoza has added boldly an attribute to God, which in the course of the history of Christianity and western metaphysics, has never been ascribed to the Godhead, viz., material extension. This amplification is much more far-reaching than the void spatiality Newton added to the immaterial God, for in Spinoza, we have to confront not just the spatialization of the deity and the divinization of free space, but more radically, the materialization of God and the divinization of the material universe. God and world simply are interlocked, and to this interlocked reality the spinozistic believer is expected to emotionally relate in a covenant-like mutuality with the God/Cosmos. On a prima facie consideration, one can hardly call this a bilateral covenant since the God/Cosmos has no personal face even though "It" arouses feelings of deep gratitude in the one who has come to love the universe with an intuitive intellectual love. Strictly speaking, however, it is also not a unilateral arrangement just set up by naturalistic mystics eager to stretch out their arms to touch a partner who has no proper face. Although God/Nature does not seem to return any gesture of affection, "It" is very active in this relationship, for what seems to be a unilateral act of worship by human beings is in fact a deep response to the life-giving forces of the cosmos which are both divine and material, and embrace us all. We have to wrestle with mystical theology but of a very strange kind, one which has incorporated the universe into God. Does this mysticism ennoble Spinoza? I would say yes in so far as he succeeded in offering a pattern of religiosity that is an imaginative yet rational synthesis of cold science and effusive self-surrender, though this synthesis was overshadowed by the 17th-century scientists' staunch mechanistic conception of the world. Does it also expose Spinoza to criticism? Yes, in so far as the recent collapse of the mechanistic conception of the world necessitates a revision of his second and third kind of knowledge without, however, demolishing their basic paradigm, the mutual inclusion of God and world.

5. Cosmic Religiosity at the End of the 20th Century

In the previous sections, we have mainly explored the changes in the attributes of God that took place in the 17th century. The result is a "status of the question" which allows us to address the religious situation at the end of the 20th century, at least as regards the cosmic God-representations. Indeed, by way of conclusion and prospect, we can ask the question as to which type of God-conception is going to stir religious feelings and to have a future in scientific milieux: Descartes' and Leibniz's deistic God, Newton's Old Testament God, Lord of the universe, or Spinoza's impersonal yet praiseworthy God/Nature? To give a conclusive answer to this question, more research will have to be done, though one can discern already some general trends that are going to be decisive for a cosmic religiosity of the future. Let us try to list them.

1. New Trends in Cosmic Religiosity

First of all, it is a remarkable fact that, nowadays, scientists – astrophysicists and specialists in quantum physics and thermodynamics – prove more sensitive to religious questions than they were some decades ago. Some of them even set out to theologize on the origin of the universe and on the meaning of our lives in the whole evolutionary cosmos. They do so either from the background of the history of theo-cosmology or from that of a particular religious tradition, usually the Judaeo-Christian tradition, although some also turn to other traditions like Buddhism and aboriginal religions. The taboo on scientists, which prevented them from calling themselves religious, is something they themselves are increasingly recognizing as an illusion.

Second, the new interest in religious questions in scientific milieux has not been primarily aroused by the churches but by new discoveries in science itself. The scientific community is presently engaged in a search for new paradigms; this has implications for our understanding of the meaning of our lives in the cosmos. The 17th-century clockwork model is slowly being replaced by the paradigm of the world as a living organism. Let us dwell a bit longer on this point.

The debate at the level of a global *Weltanschauung* pivots around the question whether or not classical Newtonian science is fully adequate as regards explaining the behaviour of *all* the phenomena in the world. The major point of critique levelled against it is that it is still caught up in a static, formal, and in a sense, passive understanding of reality. The universal laws employed to grasp the physical properties tend to freeze the vital impulses of life. Under the constraints of predictability, imposed by the general laws, the creative occurrences of phenomena happen to be reduced to the shadowy existence of interacting cogs within the operation of the world machine. This raises the question concerning the true picture of the world. Can this true picture be offered by a science that deprives the very occurrences in nature of their spontaneous and historical character? Seventeenth-century science focused on motion, and in order to formulate the universal laws of dynamics, it had to carry out a lot of mechanical reductions. "The laws of change, of time's impact on nature, are expressed in terms of the characteristics of trajectories", which are paths whose mathematically determined lines and curves can be displayed in graphs. This means that "every thing is given" and that nothing is happening crucially, for "the basic characteristics of trajectories are *lawfulness*, *determinism*, and *reversibility*"[44]. The unrolling of the system is in a sense reversible, and can be looked at as going backward even in time.

Critics of modern science see in this systematic reversibility of a series of states the very symbol of the "strangeness" of the world described by dynamics. Today's return to the particular histories occurring in nature has been inaugurated by various branches science: biology first, and then chemistry and quantum physics. Biology, as a science of life, always has been somewhat reluctant to reduce the emergence of a ramified variety of species to just reversible mechanical processes. Reluctance, however, is certainly not the same as possessing proofs. The proofs were obtained in the course of the debate in quantum physics in the thirties. Here it became evident that the deterministic and reversible laws broke down at the level of quanta. Measurements carried out in this domain disturbed the determinism of the law, for in quantum physics, "one can never be exactly sure of both the position and the velocity of a particle; the more accurately one knows the one, the less accurately one can know the other"[45]. If you measure a particle's velocity (or acceleration), then its position becomes unpredictable, and vice versa, if you measure its changing position, then the velocity becomes uncertain. This implies that the classical approach, which claimed to know the velocity (and the acceleration) of a state *at a given position* and deduced from it the behaviour of the whole dynamic system, is just crumbling down at the level of quantum measurement. The measurement *forces* aspects of the process to act in an *unlawful* manner, and thus initiates a randomness in it and an irreversible arrow of time; the quantum occurrences can no longer be read forward and backward automatically.

The existence of randomness and choice in nature turns out to be one of the basic discoveries of quantum physics. At this level, scientific research can only work with statistical probabilities and not with the laws

44. I. PRIGOGINE and I. STENGERS, *Order out of Chaos. Man's New Dialogue with Nature*, London, 1985, p. 60.

45. *Ibidem*, p. 199.

of iron predictability. Nature appears to be much more unpredictable than what classical science has believed it is, for at a *micro-level*, its basic elements seem to be endowed with the creative capability of making multiple possible choices instead of being forced just to act in the same way always. The laws of classical science are, in a sense, workable only at the *macro-level* of nature and in circumstances where the environment is sufficiently stable, whereas elsewhere nature is full of mysteries.

Replace quantum measurement by interaction with other elements in nature, and the mysterious breeding of novelty shows up again. In the field of chemistry, it is particularly the second law of thermodynamics that calls attention to the occurrence of irreversible reactions, which again confirms the importance of the arrow of time. This law says that, in the aftermath of the heat that a system is producing, emitting, and dissipating, that selfsame system's state of disorderly molecular vibrations and collisions is bound to continuously increase. This increase in disorder is technically called an increase in *entropy*. To define the entropy state of a system, one has to measure the portions of a system's total energy which are not available for making the system work. The second law of thermodynamics says that each system that works is at the same time losing energy and that this loss eventually brings it to a state of instability or non-equilibrium. The increase of disorder is irreversible, and marks thus an arrow of time. This, however, is only one side of the coin. The other is that, under certain circumstances, a system that has reached a far-from-equilibrium state might begin to interact with its environment in such a way that a new type of order emerges from it. Thus, "entropy is not merely a downward slide towards disorganization. Under certain circumstances, entropy itself becomes the progenitor of order", for the far-from-equilibrium state joins hands with processes of "randomness, and openness that lead to higher levels of organization, such as dissipative structures"[46]. Indeed, "we know that far from equilibrium, new types of structures may originate spontaneously. In far-from-equilibrium conditions we may have transformation from disorder, from thermal chaos, to order. New dynamic states of matter originate, states that reflect the interaction of a given system with its surroundings. We have called these new structures dissipative structures to emphasize the constructive role of dissipative (thermal) processes in their formation"[47]. The discovery of the arrow of time seriously questions the deterministic picture of the world that modern positivism inherited from Newton's universal laws. It opens up the possibility of marvelling again at the unexpected creative events that emerge from the womb of nature.

46. A. TOFFLER, *Science and Change*, in I. PRIGOGINE and I. STENGERS, *Order out of Chaos* (n. 44), XI-XXVI, p. XXI.

47. I. PRIGOGINE and I. STENGERS, *Order out of Chaos* (n. 44), p. 12.

If we have delved slightly into the details of the new paradigm – the discovery of randomness in nature – we have done this to show that scientists are indeed prepared to engage in a new dialogue with religion. Now, if we look at the cultural situation, it is clear that the breakthrough of the new paradigm up till now has not yet led to a proper theological reflection on God and Its relation to the world. Rather, what is taking place is a vivid interest in worship in the form of ecstasy, dance, and celebration. The dance of the quanta invites expressive utterances in worship as a sacramental way to communicate with the hidden source of creativity in the universe. From worship, hopeful cosmic mystics await a reconstruction of their emotional impulses and also the awakening of a holistic awareness. In this light, they like to envisage the immemorial cosmic evolution that eventually led to the emergence of an emotional intellect like ours capable of celebrating life. The new worshipping communities long for the integration of the remembrance of the history of the cosmos into their usual patterns of salvation history. In the domain of spirituality, tentative approaches to this cosmic integration have been worked out by Thomas Berry, and Matthew Fox in the United States[48].

This new situation poses a challenge to the Christian reflection on worship, for in the wake of widespread antropocentrism in Western culture, the liturgical renewal neglected the animating force of cosmic awareness. True, Vatican II initiated an openness towards the world of humanity and their social needs, yet it failed to properly discern those signs of the times that, in the sixties, have been already pointing to the breakthrough of a cosmic consciousness that has come to the fore eventually in the "Aquarian Conspiracy" and in "New Age" movements. In the meantime, a significant number of scientists who are engaged in the study of the basic patterns of life, tell us that, in order for the human beings to come in touch again with their deepest self and the inmost creative force called "God", they need the *mediation* of cosmic celebration. If one may ask, is there an experience of grace as overwhelming as the witness of and the self-surrender to the continual cosmic interplay of indeterminacy and form, of chaotic flux and startling emergence of new order, which in so many events in nature result in irreversible leaps of creativity? Grace it certainly is, and this is further effected when the "human observer" begins to realize that the interplay between randomness and ordered form in nature is simply part also of one's own existence. In order to behold the astonishing life-giving events in nature and to be affected by them, one ought oneself to be alive, not subjugated by the law which cannot vivify, as St. Paul says.

We theologians and perhaps the teaching office of the Church should examine our consciences to see whether or not we are still captives of

48. T. BERRY, *The Dream of the Earth*, San Francisco, 1988; B. SWIMME and T. BERRY, *The Universe Story. A Celebration of the Unfolding of the Cosmos*, San Francisco, 1992.

17th-century science with its unchangeable laws and meticulously immutable God. Grace as a gift of life and as a vitalizing force is laid out eventfully in the basic structures of the universe. Thus, should not the experience of empowerment by grace be given a stronger emphasis in our liturgies? Should we not look at the cosmos, and at our lives in it, as the sacramental manifestation of God's vivifying generosity? If, in theological parlance, the eucharist is seen as the celebration of the self-giving of God in the self-giving of Christ, is it not imperative to include in this insight the emotional commemoration of how the cosmos itself is just one grandiose spectacle of the self-giving of the Creator and the outpouring of the Spirit in so many creative events?

2. Neo-Spinozism or Classical Theism?

In this light, we can broach now the question: what valid alternative does Christianity have to offer to both deism and spinozism? Indeed, we can limit our investigation to just these two branches of theo-cosmology since they are setting the stage for further discussions among scientists. The present landscape of cosmology is mainly populated by neo-deists and neo-spinozists.

The neo-deists are those who, like Stephen Hawking and Paul Davies, try to reconstruct the computer design of God's mind before It dared to create the best of all possible worlds. More in particular, they want to uncover the magic formula that God or the cosmic astrophysical intellect must have infused into the "chemistry" of the early universe. Such a fundamental formula, regardless of the emergence of life and the uncertain final product of the continuing expansion of the universe, would still imply that the universe is just a self-sufficient clockwork. If the neo-deists would succeed in reconstructing – in the form of a Grand Unified theory – the fine-tuned initial conditions that account for the early formation of the universe, they think they would be able to know the "mind of God". Hawking is explicit in this matter: "If we find the answer to that (viz. why it is that we and the universe exist), it would be the ultimate triumph of human reason – for then we would know the mind of God"[49]. Now, in the best tradition of deism, to know the mind of God amounts to declaring God redundant.

Other scientists profess spinozism in different shades. Einstein was one of them. This is not surprising because he himself dismantled the absolute co-ordinates of space and time, which for Newton, formed the sensory organ of the immaterial God. Ever since Einstein, the world is no longer static but caught up in processes of evolution; its space is being formed by matter in explosive expansion, though the expansion is not going to be indefinite. Einstein, thus, came to rest in the heart of the cosmos, while marvelling at the continuous exchange that takes place

---

49. S. HAWKING, *A Brief History of Time*, London, 1988, p. 185.

between energy and matter measured against the velocity of light. From this vantage-point, he can be assigned to Spinoza's second and third kind of knowledge, for he acknowledged the determinations of the laws of nature – reformulated now in the new conception of space-time continuum – and the baffling, sublime effects thereof in the concrete history of the cosmos, as we find it described in the classical exposition of the Big Bang Theory.

Later generations of spinozists espouse totally different shades in their abandonment of the overall deterministic conception of nature. Like Spinoza, they go on ascribing the attribute of material extension to the deity – thus "naturalizing" God and "divinizing" nature – yet at the same time, they depart from his mechanistic presuppositions. This already brings their second way of knowing – the knowledge of the wonderful interactions in nature – to the threshold of the third way of knowing, the ecstasy of what it means to live in the womb of Mother Earth. The patriarchal God-representation Spinoza inherited from Moses Maimonides is replaced now by motherly images.

This transition can be observed in Whitehead's sketch of the caring God, the God of love of the New testament which has replaced the Old Testament ruler to which Newton attached so much importance. In his *Process and Reality*, he states that (besides the Aristotelian, Caesarian, and Hebrew God) "there is however in the Galilean origin of Christianity yet another suggestion, which does not very well fit with any of the three main strands of thought. It does not emphasize the ruling Caesar, or the ruthless moralist, or the unmoved mover. It dwells upon the tender elements in the world, which slowly and in quietness operate by love"[50]. This tenderness is also visible in the new scientific approach put forward by Prigogine and Stengers in their book "*La nouvelle alliance*" (the English version, *Order out of Chaos*). The study of nature, they say, allows us to enter into a new covenantal relationship with the universe, whose elements can no longer be "objectivized" and "frozen" into automatons placed over and against the life world of people or anaesthetized for scientists to force upon them the method of experimental inference and generalization. No, the present generation of scientists are beginning to see that they themselves, with their emotions and minds, are part of a living cosmos, which displays the characteristics of a living organism one has to approach with respect and empathy even as a scientist. We and the universe are one family, united with one another beyond the dualism of mind and body, for nature has made so many decisive and irreversible steps to make possible, by way of a grandiose accident as it were, the emergence of intelligent beings like us. This makes us wonder relentlessly where this creativity and this motherly concern of nature

50. A.N. WHITEHEAD, *Process and Reality: An Essay in Cosmology* (1929), New York, 1969, p. 404.

for us comes from? The biochemist Rupert Sheldrake shares this organic view, and crowns it by stating that the religions have always known of this bond with nature. He says, "As soon as we allow ourselves to think of the world as alive, we recognize that a part of us knew this all along. It is like emerging from winter into a new spring. We can begin to reconnect our mental life with our own direct intuitive experience of nature. We can begin to participate in the spirits of sacred places and times. We can see that we have much to learn from traditional societies who have never lost their sense of connection with the living world around them"[51].

Has Christianity a valid alternative to these two options, viz., deism and neo-spinozism (or should we call it "revised theism" as process thinkers do)? As far as this question is concerned, we would suggest that Christianity, strictly speaking, has no proper cosmological system. In the history of theology, it often borrowed cosmological models from the surrounding culture: from Plato and Aristotle in antiquity and the Middle Ages and from 17th-century scientific cosmologies in the past centuries. Yet in appropriating basic elements from these cosmologies, Christianity was also watchful in deciding as to which type of cosmology it was going to affiliate herself. For in spite of its lack of a technical cosmology, it had its proper theological axioms such as the *creatio ex nihilo* (which underlines that the whole Being of the universe depends on God's Being, the fountain-head of all created things) and the continuous creation (God sustains the universe in its becoming). These theological axioms served, in practice, to purify extant cosmologies and to fill them with a Christian content. One ought only to think of Aquinas' substitution of Aristotle's cosmic intelligences with angels.

Now, one may ask whether or not in modern times Christian theism has sided too much with cosmologies that propounded a purely external God-Creator, such as the Newtonian Pantokratoor, who imposes his will everywhere in space and time. Has theism also succeeded in keeping away from the pitfall of deism: God as the mathematical intellect of the world? What one reads in 19th-century handbooks of apologetics, about God's design being apparent in the constant behaviour of the laws of nature, is in fact very close to the idea of a God clockmaker, who is recognized in the perfect functioning of the clockwork.

Yet why should Christian theism place so heavy an emphasis on God's external transcendence? Why not approximate the unfathomable mystery of the Creator's generous self-communication, from the stimulating effects that self-communication has on the startling sequences of creativity that one can observe in the immemorial epigenesis of the cosmos, i.e., "in the genuinely new forms of reality that appear at various stages

51. R. SHELDRAKE, *The Rebirth of Nature. The Greening of Science and God*, London, 1990, p. 188.

in the history of nature"[52]. Has not Christian theism been too much on the defensive with respect to cosmologies that affirm a covenant-like bond between the active history of the evolution of the cosmos and God's immanence in the world? In this light, I would rather plead for a certain appropriation of neo-spinozism or revised theism, i.e., of cosmologies that, compared to former cosmologies, stress a greater "inclusive" unity of the Creator and the material universe, though these cosmologies of course will have to be cleansed of the determinisms of 17th-century science. Instead of methodologically starting from God's transcendence to define what divine immanence means, one should reverse the order and undertake to worship the "first hidden cause" from "within" one's perception of God's internal working "in the heart of nature"[53] and in the whole extension of the universe. This way, one will come in touch with God's *kabod* in creation, which in Jewish thinking, has something material about it, and which also draws us to the "illuminating darkness" of the deity. On the basis of their own conviction, Christians may complement this view by adding that God's material *kabod* bears the New Testament seal of the Logos: self-giving, communion, and love.

Heilige-Geeststraat 74/6   Georges DE SCHRIJVER s.j.
B-3000 Leuven

52. T. PETERS, *Preface*, in IDEM (ed.), *Cosmos as Creation. Theology and Science in Consonance*, Nashville, 1989, p. 21.

53. R.J. RUSSEL, *Cosmology, Creation, Contingency*, in T. PETERS (ed.), *Cosmos as Creation* (n. 52), 177-210, p. 182.

GOD BEYOND THE SEDUCTION OF DEISM

As the title of my article suggests, I will first examine deism, with a mind as free as possible; then I will consider the reasons for going beyond, for confessing that God is beyond.

Deism

Prof. Willaert focused his theological symposium on the central object of theology. For as Thomas Aquinas states in the beginning of the *Summa theologiae*, theo-logy is the science of the divinity of God. To say who God is, first consists of letting God manifest his divinity. We cannot dissociate the methodology and the object of our study. Methodology means the systematic way we follow towards that which we study. It consists of making clear the way God manifests himself, or to say it with Heidegger's definition of phenomenology, adapted to theology, to permit God to manifest himself as the God who shows – and eventually, who tells – who he is.

How does God become a phenomenon for us so that we know what the right meaning-content is of the word 'God'? It is with respect to this most central question that deism has been a major event in our western civilization. For it is not only a historical fact. Since its historical formation in the 18th century, it remained a seductive and still conquering conception. The confrontation with deism consequently is a major task for theology.

Forms of Deism

According to its etymology, 'deism', derived from the Latin *deus*, is equivalent to theism (derived from the Greek *Theos*, God). Historically, however, the name deism has been given to English religious writers of the 17th-18th centuries; then to the so-called enlightened philosophers, French (Diderot, Voltaire) and German (Lessing). In England, the original major deistic work (of Lord Herbert) recognized some religious conceptions as fundamental, innate in the mind, and God-given by nature from the beginning of time: the belief in a supreme being, in the need for his worship, in virtuous life as the most desirable form of worship, in the necessity of repentance, and in reward and punishment in the next world. These fundamental religious beliefs, they thought, had already been the beliefs of the first humans. On this basis, different religions and sects developed. They are modifications and often erruptions of the natural, basic religion.

Not all deists maintain all these 'natural' beliefs. Some reject the immortality of the soul, some also the belief in a divine providence in the moral order, and some only maintain a belief in a Creator God... For some, this expression does not involve the idea of a personal God.

One may call deism a philosophical religious belief. From the beginning of the history of philosophy, there has been a reciprocal attraction between religion and philosophy, between christian theology and philosophy. Religion of course came first and it gave philosophy the idea of God. Religion presents an all-encompassing scheme of reference, a map of the world and for human existence, and a set of moral laws. This surely is the case of biblical religion. It tells the origin of all beings, proposes universal principles of ethical righteousness, and announces a universal ultimate finality. We can say that such a religion foreshadows what a philosophy can dream of: 'foreshadows', for religion effects in its own language and in concrete signs and symbolic behaviours what is characteristic of the human mind and what philosophy will elaborate: the capacity of considering things from a transcendental and universal point of view. This capacity renders the human mind never fixed in a conceptual prison nor in a system of needs and need-satisfactions.

When the human mind has acquired this transcendental capacity, why should it still depend on religion?

So to me, it seems there are three steps in the process of the reciprocal attraction between theology and philosophy; these three steps are not necessarily successive in history.

1. When the scientific or philosophical mind encounters religion, it tries to conceptualize and to express the contents of religion in concepts the rational mind is acquainted with, or can somewhat understand. Thus the christian God-idea is conceived in philosophical terms such as: the highest essence, the highest being (esse), the full act of being, the highest spirit, the good itself, the infinite, the first and the final cause...

The second step is the development of the rational proofs of the existence of this God. Allow me here just to mention this: What is interesting in the context of the study of deism is that Descartes was already convinced that the idea of God is innate, as the idea of the Infinite. One sees here a clear progression of rationalism: the idea of God belongs to the natural spontaneous activity of reason.

The third step will be the statement that this natural, rational God-idea is the essential and sufficient basis for religion and that theology (or christian religion) does not add anything fundamental or important. We have witnessed here in Leuven the process of deism repeating itself years ago. One of our professors of philosophy was convinced that he could really prove the existence of the personal God, Creator, with the high divine qualities (good, just, non-violence), and that he could prove the immortality of the soul. He was so convinced of this natural theology that he also convinced some students that they did not need to believe in God anymore.

When philosophy now makes the religious God-idea its own, then human reason imposes on it its own standards. In other words, the tendency then prevails to redeem rationally the religious content of the God-idea. This tendency prevailed with the development of the critical mind in all domains (critical studies of religious texts, etc.). Also in other respects, the critical mind fostered a growing sense of intellectual mastery and of affective and moral autonomy. Deism has been the product of this enlightened critical mind. And, as I have already insisted, the religious deistic conception persists, spreads, and is probably prevalent in our time in the West. Some weeks ago, there was an interview on television with the famous astrophysicist of Cambridge, S. Hawking, the man who carries out scientific work while completely paralyzed, confined to his armchair, and surrounded by medical technology similar to intensive care. At the end the interviewer asked him: do you believe in God? His answer: "Not in a God after death I will meet and who will judge me... But for me as an astrophysicist God is evident". Who or what is this God? Is it more than some principle immanent within the cosmos? Deism often ends up with such a God-belief. Of course, the word belief is inadequate here. When the BBC interviewed the famous psychologist C.G. Jung, they asked him the same question: do you believe in God? Jung's answer was typical and more right: "I do not believe, I know". When the term belief is used in deism, it is in the sense of a somewhat uncertain knowing *that*, or in the sense of an experience, which also is a form of knowing.

2. Deism is a post-christian, so-called return to natural religion on the basis of a natural theology. In other words, natural theology is no longer the reasonable philosophical basis of theology, but becomes the science of God and the exclusive basis of religion. Being post-christian, deism does not return to polytheism and animism; the biblical monotheism remains the reference. In its opposition to biblical religion, deism then identifies itself by some negative characteristics.

1) Refusal of religious authorities. The critics of the authoritarian and repressive clergy and of churches which rejected the modern world, encouraged the development of a more fundamental attitude: the claim to be autonomous in very personal matters of religion. The word 'dogma' consequently loses its theological meaning and becomes a sociological and psychological negative term evoking ideological authority and repression. The deist generally also rejects the religious authority of the Bible and the Gospel. We can observe this characteristic of deism in the contemporary mentality if we listen to the way many speak about the Bible. They repeat a new theoretical cliché. Each civilization, they say, has its great narratives that overlay its representations and sentiments. Our civilization developed under the reign of the great biblical narrative; this became the myth of the West. Our time has lost its narrative, one then adds. Now if we read the Bible, of course we read narrative texts next

to prophetic, poetic, and speculative ones. But to interpret the Bible just as a cultural narrative means denying *a priori*, with an intellectual cliché, its specific character, which even an unprejudiced, unbelieving reader can recognize. The Bible is a living whole. To be sure, it involves a pluralism of conceptions and behaviours that are evolving, changing, and progressing. But it is a whole because there is force of attraction working in it, not the force of a hidden memory of a primitive, pure natural religion but that of the progressive revelation of the living God. Because of this focus on God coming to humanity, the biblical texts make a striking authoritative claim on the reader. Throughout all kinds of features belonging to all literature, there is a constant violent claim in the biblical texts, a claim that is coherent with the conviction to proclaim an unheard truth and an unseen reality: the truth and reality of the living God. In this sense the Bible is a violent book. It has the tone of the incisive word of Jesus: "No man, having put his hand to the plough, and looking back, is fit for the Kingdom of God" (Luke 9,62). One may believe or not, but one cannot read the Bible in the way one reads the mythological stories of Heracles or the tale of Eros Plato invented, or the Odyssey[1]. I do not need to assure you that what I say has nothing in common with biblical fundamentalism.

2) The rejection of divine revelation follows from the rejection of religious authority, for revelation passes through authorized witnesses. It is typical for the Bible that its narrative surface coincides with the deeper content: the history of God's progressive self-revelation. The prophets reinterpret the patriarchs and the former history; Jesus reinterprets the prophets; the first christians again interpret. The story of the Emmauspilgrims illustrates the revelation-procedure. A phenomenologist would speak of self-manifestation: God becoming a phenomenon through human thought. A psychologist would talk of the invention of the God-idea. These are also the ways that deists talk. But revelation is more specific than manifestation, and revelation is radically different from invention. The prophets, and more explicitly Jesus, speak on behalf of God and claim divine authority for their messages. God is permanently present and absent in this revelation, present as acting presence and absent as the permanent future Other. Consequently, the history that makes the Bible a whole and which is the ground for speaking of *a* book, is the progressive history of God's newness within the world. Now rational thought resists the idea of an unforeseeable newness. This is an *a priori* conviction in the rational modern mind. The cosmos is an evolving system; human civilizations are in process of transformations. But these are changes of the system itself, changes reason can retrospectively reconstruct and understand. The mind meets with *a priori* distrust the

---

1. I agree with the thesis defended by the biblical scholar James BARR, *Reading the Bible as Literature*, in *Bulletin of the John Rylands Library* 56 (1973-74) 10-33.

idea of revelation as a really new divine reality. In this respect there is a platonic trend in the human mind. Is not the biblical story of the first paradise partly also the expression of a mind that tends to deny the manifestation of the newness, of the event in the strict sense? God's presence with humans, happiness, immortality: for the paradise myth all is given from the beginning, and history is only the reparation of a loss. That is also the way in which Freud constantly speaks. Revelation as God's manifestation within human history — this is a disturbing idea for the rationally enlightened mind.

3) The rejection of an interventionist God is another aspect of deistic rationalism. Intervention and self-revelation are of course twin ideas. Intervention is larger; it also evokes God's acting in historical events, in persons, in miracles, and in belief mysteries like the resurrection of Jesus. For the modern mind, the world is a system in which no supernatural forces intervene. Most people feel very uneasy with the idea of a God intervening. This seems to them to be a relapse into old magic. Even among subjects who explicitly confess a christian belief in God, the idea of God's intervention in history got a very low score in one of our researches in psychology of religion.

4) Deism involves an inclusive oecumenism. This means a conception of religion that interprets all religions as particular, culturally determined models of expressing and representing the few fundamental religious contents, essentially the God idea. Wilfred Smith, an American philosopher of religion and a typical deistic oecumenist, defends, for example, the following thesis: "While the various religious communities of the world have differed in belief, they have not essentially differed in faith"[2]. But, says Smith, when they confuse belief and faith, then they are exclusive of one another, and are eventually intellectually, socially, and politically intolerant. Faith is the capacity to be involved in the spiritual religious orientation of the self... To pretend to have the divine truth is intolerant ethnocentricity. All religions are different viewpoints on the same divine or God, whatever that may be — that is not important.

This inclusive oecumenism is of course the consequence of the above-mentioned characteristics, however it has its special affective flavour of universalistic, democratic, and anti-authoritarian disposition. In deistic oecumenism there arises an affective irritation with respect to the idea of meaningful differences. The language usage itself expresses the *a priori* reduction of differences: one speaks of Jewish, Christian, Islamic, Greek, Hindu myths. Actually no scholar of comparative religion would hold such oecumenical views. Unbeliever and believer scholars alike stress, for example the profound differences between the monotheist biblical God and the gods of the classic Greek religion, who are not really personal but somewhat personified representations of the neutral

---

2. *Faith and Belief*, Princeton, 1979.

divine. Biblical monotheism is exclusive; on the contrary, the tendency to monotheism in the ancient Roman or Greek religion is inclusive. Deism also is inclusive, for in deism human beings and their world are the standard of religious truth.

5) There is the spontaneous tendency to adopt the cosmological model for conceiving of divine transcendence and for opposing it to anthropomorphism. A new sense of space and time brought about the representation of divine greatness in opposition to the idea of a personal God. I am convinced that in this respect a deep-rooted existential awareness is involved that is very important. It is however difficult to analyse this because it does not belong to the conscious philosophical ideas. Let us reflect on the following text of the philosopher Karl Jaspers, a text expressing his personal conviction: "When persons addresses the divinity in prayer, this divinity becomes for him a Thou with whom, lost in solitude, they would establish communication. The divinity is then for them a personal figure... However, the authentic consciousness of the transcendence of the divine resists thinking of the absolute God as a person". (Philosophie, trad. Hersch, Berlin, 1989, p. 741; my translation in English). Of course, I would say: personal, not a person. According to Jaspers, humanity today feels lost as almost an accidental figure in an unthinkable extended cosmos, a system expanding itself for billions of years, a system that through a wonderful complex combination of lawful regularities and chance-happenings produced somewhere the human being. The divine should be conceived as in harmony with the grandeur of the cosmic time and space and the lawful regularities, and not as a personal ego who speaks, not as an ego who listens to praying humanity, that is, not at the image of the insignificant little and lost person. You probably know a famous statement of S. Freud: "In the course of centuries the *naïve* self-love of men has had to submit to two major blows at the hands of science. The first one was when they learned that our earth was not the centre of the universe but only a tiny fragment of a cosmic system of scarcely imaginable vastness... The second blow fell when biological research destroyed man's supposedly privileged place in creation and proved his descent from the animal kingdom...". And Freud adds: "But human megalomania will have suffered its third and most wounding blow from the psychological research of the present time..." etc. (SE XVI, 285: Introductory Lectures XVIII, concl.). This statement written in 1916 now sounds a bit naïve – sit venia verbo! – Humanity feels diminished but at the same time is proud of being the top of the evolution of life. And one acquired a new sense of greatness in this knowledge of the vastness of time and space in which one is lost and of the depth of the psychic processes. But one thinks of God with cosmic schemes in mind. So did Aristotle. And this drives one toward a splitting and opposition between the ideas of divine grandeur (transcendence) and a personal God.

From the beginning, deism tended to integrate religious belief and science of nature. The idea of a design in the cosmos – and evolution – has been a major argument in 'natural' religious knowledge. The enthusiasm that Teilhard de Chardin raised after the war in some milieux, christian and deistic, was due to his particular poetic-mystical way of integrating christian religion and science by means of a comprehensive religious-scientific teleological scheme. I fear that the accommodation between the contents of christian belief and the scientific worldview only convinces the christians who try to convince the deists.

6) Finally, I will briefly mention a last point: the fact that many feel the christian doctrine of salvation through the sacrificial death of Jesus to be a repellent conception of God, repellent because of what Bultmann called the barbarian image of divine cruelty. It seems (and is!) absurd to speak of a divine loving Father requiring the death of his divine son out of love for sinful humanity and as a condition for forgiveness. A clear, serene, natural belief in a gentle creator seems more respectful. But the gentle smile of this Creator is soon absorbed in the radiance of cosmic energy.

I presented what I could read and hear from the side of deism. A return to a supposed natural religion, they say. We could also call it a basic religion, as you have basic English, and some years ago, psychological writings about 'the basic personality'. At any rate, it is a religion without mythical, dogmatic, and ritual mysteries; the only true mystery is that of the cosmos, and the recognition of a God is the response to it. Jesus is the marvelous poetic teacher of this natural religion. But ultimately humanity does not need the teacher.

The conception of a well-ordered universe has been shaken since the rational optimism of the first deists. There are those who see the cosmos rather as a builder's yard, even as a lumber camp without purpose and order, the appropriate site for a society disorganized by the power of evil. Since the finger of God is no more perceptible in creation, the face of the benevolent intelligent creator wanes. This is a supplementary argument against the religion of a personal God.

The legacy of deism is this: while the main note of public opinion at the end of the twentieth century is still a confession of God-belief, the word God is often used without attaching to it the proper meaning which the word 'God' had in biblical monotheism. Thus, many who in recent sociological enquiries say they believe that God exists, interpret the word deistically. And they also refer to the two natural sources for what is for them belief that God exists. The more scientific minds attest to a sense of awe and contemplative thought in the face of the greatness, the impressive complexity, and the marvelous lawful structures and processes in nature. Others are more aesthetically sensitive to wonder and beauty in nature, in art, and in religious poetry and iconography. Deists retrieve in their own manner the fundamental ways towards the divine, possibly the divine creator, already traced by Plato and Aristotle.

Beyond

Deism is seductive for many reasons. It presents itself as the natural religion of all sensible persons, a religion cleaned and freed from sacred authorities on human existence, a religion confident in a benevolent God, or a religion without God but still having a spiritual openness in life, a religion without sectarianism but universally oecumenical, a religion that can adopt almost any kind of religious texts as symbolic expressions that give a poetic touch to belief without divine mysteries, and a religion with a scientific undertone.

Why go beyond? Intellectual honesty should ask that question. I would ask the question here from the point of view of the christian believer. My interest here is theological. I expect from the clarification of the discrepancy between deism and christian God-belief that it will lead to more insight into God and into humanity, both considered together. I insist upon considering together the human person and God.

1. I start by addressing to deism some critical questions. Heidegger, and Merleau-Ponty who was influenced by him, have shown that an anthropocentric shift took place in our way of thinking. This shift influenced the God-idea at its foundation. Until the modern times indeed, the christian God-idea was the norm; the endeavour of metaphysics was to enlighten the pre-given God-idea theoretically with ontological concepts. The divinely revealed God-idea had its supra-rational authority in itself. Christian belief thus preserved human thought from a narrowing anthropocentrism. Whatever may be the particular historical and sociological forces that shaped the deistic turn, a common process and passion is at work in the features I analysed: in the rejection of revelation, of religious authorities, and of the belief in the intervening God. The anthropocentric shift of interest and thought is therein an underlying driving force. Only what humanity, as the conscious centre of the cosmos, can experience, observe, and think, is true and real. Only what has utility and function for humanity in the world, is valuable. In this perspective, the idea of God or of the divine must be submitted to the natural conceptions of humanity as being in the world. God does not make a difference. Deism intends to be the natural religion of humanity as we are naturally: a religion within the limits of reason and of religious experience. Historically, the deistic religion of course never did exist before deism. It is a cultural conquest or product of modern humanity. Natural, however, is here first opposed to supernatural factors in christian belief-religion. God's historical self-revelation indeed does not belong to the world as world, and is not a part of the religiosity of humanity as being in the world. But in face of deism, the believer expresses his astonishment: if God is really God, why could he not supernaturally reveal himself and intervene in creation without disturbing its immanent laws?

A general and more obvious reason for opposing the historical supernatural divine initiative is the idea that the belief in supernatural events would disturb the concept of a lawful world, a concept humanity has attained through centuries of civilization. This attainment and conquest is the pride of educated people; they suspect the religious idea of supernatural divine initiatives to be the denial of this conquest. They feel humiliated by it. As many say, there is not a rational or theoretical, but an affective conflict. Actually the christian tradition had and still may have a problem with recognizing the requirements of nature in its full extent. Think of the multiple forms of belief in the intrusion of supernatural agencies within the human world: stories of visions, apparitions, miracles, stigmata, possession... There is longing and fascination for the observable supernatural, but in most of our contemporaries, there is a deep distrust with respect to any supernatural event. Hence the *a priori* conviction that forms of the so-called supernatural can and should be explained by natural factors. Deism in this sense shares in what the enlightenment calls human emancipation.

I maintain my critical remark concerning the anthropocentric shift in modern times. But I add that this shift did help christian belief to dissociate the true supernatural divine events from the mixture of christian religion and imaginary supernatural phenomena that should be explained by laws of nature ("nature" in the broad sense). I think, however, that the church did not yet appreciate to its full extent the requirements of human nature – a lot of talk and practice in the domain of rituals is too supernaturalistic. Maybe this is also a reason for the decline of ritual praxis. Deism did help us to have a right conception of God acting in history. I would go this far then in the recognition of God's intervention within history, and believe that God is immanently acting in historical processes such as the establishment of a scientific worldview and secularization. In these cultural-religious events, God's creation is coming-to-pass. God however is still hiding himself therein. For anthropology, the history of the God-idea is a part of the history of mankind. From the point of view of theology, the history of the God-idea is a part of the history of God with humanity – a history which is not a process of linear progress.

It is of course our belief in Jesus that allows us to interpret God's action in this way. Jesus reveals God to us also by the way he hides his divinity. The principle governing God's action in the world is clearly formulated in one of the earliest christian texts which St. Paul quotes: "Who, being in the form of God, did not consider equality with God something to be grasped at. But... took upon him the form of a servant, and was made in human likeness..." I do not read this text as a dogmatic text formulating the dogma of the divine pre-existence and incarnation. The text stresses, I think, the way Jesus did reveal and manifest God. Now we can better understand the deistic rejection of the supernatural when we remember the tendency in the christian tradition to present and confess a christology that, practically, does not acknowledge the full humanity of Jesus. Today on the contrary, the tendency is to reduce Jesus to a genial and marvelous religious man...

A whole anthropocentric way of thinking and evaluating tends thus to exclude *a priori* dogmatic belief. In the same way, just as in the past a cultural necessity enforced a supernaturalistic view that failed to fully recognize nature, today a cultural necessity enforces a deistic reinterpretation of the christian content of belief. Therefore I insist on the necessary critical questioning of *a priori* preconceptions. If we reflect on the idea of a God, is it not finally an absurd idea to conceive of a God who has no divine project, who is supposed to have created and then retires, who is not acting in history? It is more logical then to interpret the word God as a cipher, a code-word for an inexhaustible mystery lying within the observable word and beneath or above human existence. This is a respectable attitude. It should be clear, however, that in calling 'God' the unknowable enigma of the world, one does not add any insight. On the contrary, serious religious questioning is foreclosed and the illusion of explanation can be created. If God is not the God of biblical monotheism, the God who is personal, who has his own divine identity, what does it offer to the understanding of the world and of our existence to maintain the idea of God? What is the difference with atheism that recognizes a mystery in the world that is a beautiful wonder and a terrifying fate? Why call God this natural wonder and fate?

Some think we should reshape our God-idea, for they say it is constructed on the old medieval worldview; now it should be adapted to the new worldview as this is shaped by modern cosmology and by evolutionism. Teilhard de Chardin is of course the most sympathetic paradigm of this theological trend. God is the Omega point towards which the whole cosmic process moves, Christ is the fulfillment of the evolution, Christ is the incandescent centre of this all-encompassing process, etc... Is this language more than euphoric theological-scientific mythology? That means, is it not a language that fails to recognize the differential identity of the world and of God? It tries to bridge the difference between the history of the world and the history of God. It interprets the natural data in supernatural terms, and it often – not in Teilhard of course – will end up in interpreting the supernatural data, the divine history, in natural terms. This is the natural tendency of deism and of a theology that lets itself be fascinated by deism.

If we start from the world and from humanity, nothing in the natural processes aims at a God. If we start from the faith conviction – "I believe in God" – then we may say that the whole cosmic and human history has its finality and reaches its accomplishment in God. But then we should add: I do not see it; what I observe with my human eyes and what I understand with my reason neither support nor contradict that belief; but I believe it on the basis of God's self-revelation. If on the contrary one interprets natural phenomena in religious terms, one ends up interpreting divine history and reality in natural terms.

I will summarize these cultural-religious events in a somewhat brutal formulation. Theology integrated philosophy and constructed a bridge between theology and philosophy: the 'natural theology'. Then philosophy integrated theology and came up with a natural religion. Nature integrated the God of natural religion, and deism came up with a somewhat religious a-theism. Consequently, those who interpret christian belief in the sense of deism will end up with a kind of religious a-theism. Rather than trying to adapt the christian message to the so-called new worldview, I prefer therefore to ask critically: why are people so seduced by the deistic inclination in today's religious thought? My observations teach me that a secret fear, a fear of the nature of anxiety is aroused by the christian God-message. 'Anxiety' means a diffused, unreflective feeling of being threatened. Threatened in what sense? R. Otto, Mircea Eliade, and others have described the religious experience as awe and sense of tremendum. That is anxiety within religion. What I observe today is different: it is anxiety in the face of the uncontrollable, unforeseeable, the supernatural of the divine self-revelation. It is the anxiety of people who feel God as an intrusion in their world. When God is God, not an immanent force within the world, then humanity has to open their existence for a wholly Other coming from afar. One should ponder upon the following observation everybody can make. People who are deists, or people who interpret christian religion deistically, are convinced that they have reached what they call a mature religiosity. That is a typical idea of the enlightenment, and psychologists are fond of that word, especially when talking about religion. Often, the belief in a personal God, surely the belief in the incarnation and in the resurrection of Jesus, are evaluated as immature religion. What has this to do with maturity? Asking that critical question, you get vague answers, but they always go in the same direction: maturity is theoretical, affective, and moral mastery, i.e., independence of human persons within their world. Freud, who was a convinced enlightened atheist, was not impressed by the psychological pride of the so-called mature deistic religion. In 1928 in a letter to Marie Bonaparte he wrote: "One risks underestimating the religious sentiments among intellectuals... That stems from all the beverages we are offered under the name of religion, beverages which contain a tiny percentage of alcohol – possibly not any alcohol; however people gorge on it. After all, the old drinkers were a respectable brotherhood; but to get drunk with apple-juice is really ridiculous".

In the face of the anxiety religion awakens, there is therefore something odd and naïve when church persons address others saying that they bring 'the good news'. These words did resound with more obvious meaning for Jewish believers in God. In order to acknowledge the good message of the God of revelation, one must be intellectually and affectively free. That intellectual-affective liberation from resistance and anxiety requires a whole labour because the person is involved in it at the heart of their being.

2) While insisting sharply on the difference between the monotheistic

revelation religion and the deistic religion, I nevertheless would give natural religious experience its full right and weight. God is beyond the world of deism, but the acknowledgment of God depends on the intellectual and the aesthetic-religious experience. The acknowledgment of God requires intellectual freedom and also a positive disposition that, to some extent, conducts the mind and the emotions into the openness of the mystery at the border of the human world. The aesthetic-religious experience, which deism so positively values, is essential in establishing the disposition which enables the hearing of God's self-revelation.

Tendencies and experiences of humanity in the world break open the limits of a religion that would be kept in the confinement of reason. The wonderfully structured processes revealed by the sciences arouse the emotion of awe and admiration which moves beyond the frontiers of reason, beyond the frontiers of the world. And within the constructive dynamism of science itself, there is, as Kant has demonstrated in the second part of the *Critique of Pure Reason*, a fundamental belief, belief in reason and belief in the meaningful structure of reality. Other persons are more commonly aesthetic in their approach; they are particularly sensitive to the might and beauty in nature, in the cosmos, and in cultural forms, and they respond to it by artistic expressions of poetry, song, dance, and music. And many people are capable of both interests and experiences. That disposition and that experience do not by themselves lead to God. But the observation of our contemporaries as well as the study of comparative religion and of the history of philosophy (from Plato to Hegel and Heidegger), show us that this kind of disposition and experience is akin and connected to religious disposition. It is not accidental that, in every civilization, religion produces what we call 'works of art' (poetry, iconography, music). I wonder whether theologians, psychologists, and sociologists of religion sufficiently reflect on this impressive fact: in the countries of ideological persecution – in the nazi and the communist regimes – artistic expression had an enormous humanistic significance. Together with religion, it sustained moral resistance against a dehumanizing system.

In the aesthetic disposition and experience, one feels like a being of lack and desire, moving beyond all that is of the order of need or utility. This experience can be given by art, by the perception and observation of nature, or by disinterested scientific practice. Therein lies the affinity between the aesthetic experience and the secret heart of religious interest. The open finality of lack and desire – that is the active transcendence that makes one a human being, an ego, and which one affirms passionately in art and religion when ideologies shut one up mentally and affectively. That secret heart of lack and desire – that is what we commonly call love in the sense of *eros*. And that is not nature in the cosmic sense.

Plato connected the aesthetic experience with eros, and made eros an ascending power. In the disposition of admiration, delight, and enjoyment for the pure insight in the wondrous secrets of matter and life and humanity and for the aesthetic qualities – there, love is involved because there, humanity surpasses the utilitarian functionalistic attitude. This disposition is free from need based upon egocentric preoccupation and from egotistic striving to aggrandize one's own power. In this disposition, human persons know they are neither the origin nor the centre of their own existence, and they positively move beyond the limits of reason-controlled mastery.

As Plato has already made evident, this love does not move to a personal divine presence but to a neuter: 'the divine', a divine quality of perfection one surmises as the accomplishment of the eros-movement. Eros, admiration of beauty and veneration of what is sacred are akin. When God reveals himself as ego, he simultaneously reveals the awful and terrifying mystery and beauty as the irradiation of his personal divinity. This is the way I understand what is so fundamental in the biblical God-idea: the manifestation of God's glory, Kabod: impressive density and weigh of reality visibly irradiating as the incandescent fringe of the hidden personal God. The confession of saint Augustine, after his conversion, brings these elements together in a powerful prayer-expression: "Sero *te* amavi, pulchritudo tam antiqua et tam nova": "Late did I come to love you, beauty so old and so new". And should I remind you of the verse in which John condensed the significance of Jesus: "and we have beheld his glory (doxa)"... "*Etheasametha*": we have had and we have insight and we contemplate his glory. And you know, this is said concerning the *Word* who became flesh. John insists continuously on it: to hear allows one to have insight, to behold. It is also what Augustine stresses in the above-mentioned conversion prayer. In these words "we have beheld his glory" we hear that an endpoint is reached, not of the movement of nature, but of a finalized divine history of revelation. There, human striving, longing, desire, search, and our being moved by God who entered our world, come to a present fulfillment that is not a dead end but a presence that does not foreclose the future. As Augustine writes: (too) late, so old and so new.

As you see, I resist the preoccupation of some apologetic-minded theologians whose endeavour is to show that christian belief is useful and functional for modern humanity and for society. Some stress the psychological therapeutic utility of religion; often they follow Jung's interpretation of religion, and ultimately, many come to interpret God, Jesus' incarnation, etc, as religious symbols for a human reality. This is a modern therapeutic-minded deism, and from some readings of Drewerman, I fear this to be the direction he is going. Some stress the ethicopolitical involvement and they seem to value christian religion primarily for its socially functional contributions. That is not the thought of Gustavo Gutiérrez, the founder of liberation theology. And therefore some call him, with a light contempt, a mystical theologian. These functionalistic valuations of christian belief are new forms of deistic religion within the limits of reason. As did the original deism, they use the categories of human sciences to elaborate their theology. In this regard they are of course right. The question is what kind of anthropological and philosophical categories they adopt. Human experience and christian theology should prevent us from being entrapped in human science theories that reduce the person to a complex of vital and social needs, drives, and functions, in other words, that which is not the person as such. If God is beyond deism, it is also because he is beyond the needs, desires, and functions of humanity as well as beyond the laws of nature. God as revealing, manifesting his glory, essentially in Jesus Christ, is the open-ended fulfillment of the disinterested desire. The major contribution of christian belief to our anthropocentric culture would consequently be, contrary to the functionalistic reinterpretation of christian religion, to break open the narrowing anthropocentrism and so to safeguard true humanity.

3) Deism often tends to identify religion with ethics. In biblical religion, ethics are indeed intrinsically connected with the revelation of God. The first commandment is the basis of the other ones, and in order to accomplish the first one, one also must accomplish the others. But deism often interprets ethics as the essence of religion, and it even could disconnect ethics from religion. This leads to practical and theoretical atheism as has been observed.

My point of view today is again the theology of God. In this perspective, I would briefly consider the question of christian ethics. The question we may ask is of course whether or not there is a specific ground for christian ethics. From the point of view of philosophy – of reason – there are many grounds for ethics because the human person is made up of manifold dimensions. What is striking in the ethics of the prophets and of Jesus is that their ethics is different from ethics founded on reason. Their ethics is radical and surpasses all functional and social considerations. Their ethics surpasses the definition of humanity as being-in-the-world. In the prophetic ethics and in the ethics of Jesus, God reveals himself as the personal God, he simultaneously states the absolute personal dignity of humans, and he poses the accomplishment of his ethical commandments as conditioning his divine love. In some sense, these ethics are irrational, eventually contrary to reasonable ethics, as Freud did say. In this respect also, God explicitly reveals his divinity, that what he is. The foundation of the biblical and evangelical ethics is not reason but the will of God. This will is absolute, that is, not related to and dependent on finite goals, needs and functions.

The objection then of deism to biblical ethics is that it is based on an exterior authority, not on the authority of one's own conscience. The enlightened person no longer needs to receive ethical laws from a superior authority. That may be the philosophical viewpoint; it is neither the biblical nor the evangelical. For the will of God is creative, not only at the origin, but as the paternal vow ('voeu paternel') – to use a nice expression of Gabriel Marcel. By announcing his ethical commandments,

God places the human person in absolute personal dignity. Human dignity is not relative, dependent on social functioning or on the loss of it and on socially and psychologically determined honor or shame for bodily miseries. Therefore, christian ethics will always oppose active euthanasia.

I would use a paradoxical formulation. Christian ethics is beyond ethics, just as God is beyond the god of deists. In the deistic conception, to say that God is the authority and source of ethical imperatives, would mean denying human persons the ethical auto-nomy, which is their dignity. Nietzsche then gives his psychological interpretation: the feeble person obeys. What is distinctively prophetic and evangelical is the intrinsic connection between God's self-revelation and the divine imperatives. In other words, it is contrary to the extrinsicism deism stigmatizes. When God declares his imperatives, he reveals who and what God is for humanity and what humanity means for God, and in doing so, he reveals who God is. Within belief, there is no extrinsicism. For God bestows a new dignity upon the human person.

I would comment a moment more on this intrinsic connection. Human ethics have different sources, I think. For the human being is a multidimensional being: a citizen, has a profession and friends, is involved in a love relationship, is father or mother... Each dimension is the basis of a set of specific ethical imperatives. What is the subject as subject? Whatever may be the philosophical answer to this dreadful question, for christian belief, one thing is sure: at the moment that God declares himself as ego — Jahweh — he poses himself as absolute ego in the face of humanity. This ego-declaration is a speech-act, addressing the human "you", thus formulating a relation, thus founding the person as a relational person for God beyond the dimensions philosophical ethics can acknowledge. And God's address to humanity is universal as is creation.

Already, love leads one beyond one's being in the world, for human love is desire, eros: *searching* for what one has not. Even more, human love already includes some quality that is not eros in the sense of Plato: the bestowal of qualities on the other. But that is so irrational that neither Plato nor Aristotle could bring this feature into relief. Kierkegaard however wrote this striking formulation: love *gives* what one does not have. We can interpret this as, love gives itself. This is surely the definition of agape. Agape in the full sense therefore is divine. It is the divinity of God. Human-christian love can only be a mixture of eros and agape varying according to the situation, a mixture that cannot be codified and which therefore is charged with a dynamic uneasiness. Again, ethics is human-istic and the so-called christian ethics, as christian, is beyond ethics.

We cannot speak of God in the language of ethics. As Kierkegaard rightly writes: God cannot be virtuous. However in the western church, one is so accustomed to moralize continuously that not only in the popular vulgata the word "to preach" means to moralize but that one also speaks about God's love in moral categories. Divine love is not a virtue of God; it is the very essence of God. So God cannot not love. And love then means, to give what he is: himself.

To Conclude

I did not deal with the so-called divine qualities: good, just, almighty, eternal. As divine qualities, they are facets of God's divinity, and should be understood in this perspective. They are metaphorical language as is all language about God. And to deal with them requires an insight in the process of metaphorization and an insight into the divinity of God. In discussing with deism, I came to the statement that God is God in revealing his divinity. This revelation is a speech-act, which as such could only be historical. As a divine act, it has its authority in itself, and it can only be acknowledged as coming from the outside, the beyond of the world, introducing the divine personal presence in the world. Not the metaphysical names but 'Jahweh' is the proper divine name, says Aquinas in one text. In revealing his divine ego, God reveals visible signs as manifestation of his divinity. So if one asks the bible: what does God reveal? The answer is: his divinity, himself: Jahweh and his glory, i.e. the density, height, might, beauty, and radiance of his divinity. Revelation as speech-act that addresses humanity founds relations and dignity. It is agape. God effected, revealed and manifested all this fully in the man Jesus. For agape is very concrete and personal. Therefore, on the question who God is, I read the answer in this verse: The Word (the divine ego addressing humanity) was made flesh, and we beheld his glory.

Herbert Hooverplein 5/7   Antoon VERGOTE
B-3000 Leuven

THE GOD OF THE PHILOSOPHERS
AND THE GOD OF PASCAL

In 1974 a book appeared which was very popular and which nevertheless contained a number of gripping passages worth remembering. In *Zen
and the Art of Motorcycle Maintenance* a teacher of rhetoric, Phaedrus,
tells that once a serious student came to him with the intention to write
a 500 word essay about the United States[1]. She had trouble beginning
because she felt she had nothing to say on the subject. The teacher
suggested that she should narrow the subject to the city of Bozeman,
Montana, where she lived. This, however, did not seem to help. One
week later she came back with the somber news that she still did not
have anything to say on the subject. Then he advised her: limit your
subject to the main street in Bozeman. But that did not help either.
Again, one week later she was in a state of desperation and tears. She
really had nothing to say. The teacher then became angry and said: "You
are not *looking*. Each fact contains an infinity of hypotheses. The more
you look, the more you see". He then said: "Limit the subject to the
facade of one building on the main street in Bozeman, the Opera, and
begin with the upper left brick". One week later the student returned with
an essay of 5000 words about the facade of the Opera on the main street
of Bozeman, Montana.

1. Faith and Reason; Opinion and Science

This is one of the many anecdotes contained in the book. This passage
needs to be seen against the background of the history of philosophy and
of thought in general. What is conspicuous in this story is the depth
which is hidden in ordinary, everyday reality: the inspirational potential
of concrete details. The mind must return to earth in order to acquire new
power and to regain its zeal, an idea which also plays a large role in the
Dutch poet, Nijhoff. It is not supernatural abstractions which bring the
soul to ecstasy; it is the upper left brick in a specific facade. This is what
the student discovers after she exhausts herself in vain with higher
thoughts.

There is one dominant direction in Western philosophy which has
taught the opposite. Plato demonstrates in the *Symposium* and in the
Phaedrus how the mind, beginning with a phenomenon from visible

---

1. R. PIRSIG, *Zen and the Art of Motorcycle Maintenance*, London, 1974, p. 184 ff.

reality, can gradually ascend toward more abstract entities[2]. The soul undergoes a gradual process of learning. The lover is initially fascinated by beautiful bodies and especially one in particular. He must first learn to love all beautiful bodies and to cast aside his passion for the one body. Then he must come to the realization that the beauty of the soul has more value than all physical attraction. The third step is the insight that soul-beauty in general has more value that the one separate soul. In ascending to always higher spheres, Beauty itself is finally revealed to the lover: Beauty clean and pure, unconnected to flesh or other mortal decoration[3].

What is important is that from this point on, the world of ideas in Plato is again anchored in the idea of the Good. That is the final source of light and being. The world of true being has an aesthetic impact. It impacts knowing and conscience with its full weight of true reality. I have spoken elsewhere of this connection of the metaphysical-moral complex[4]. According to Plato's *Phaedrus*, having arrived at the summit of the cosmos, standing "on the back of heaven", the soul finds its nourishment.

It is clear that Phaedrus, the teacher of rhetoric in the book cited above, is a sort of anti-Phaedrus. His student must go the opposite direction in three steps. Her spirit is dull, without the spark of creativity, as long as the way back down from generality to the concrete is not travelled. That spiritual nourishment must be sought elsewhere was also the idea behind the foolish bees in "Het lied der dwaze bijen" by Martinus Nijhoff. They had to pay with their life, for the illusion of nourishment elsewhere. The last time says: "It snows amidst the hive". This foolish passion of the bees rightly embitters the flowers. The flowers are only restored honor in a later poem, "Tweeërlei dood" where Nijhoff, versus the poet who pursues his happiness "through infinite unsuccessful attempts and in blowing snow breathes in an ice cold light", presents a girl who wanders over the land, singing and picking flowers which she puts in a bowl at home. The torn poet then begs God that he will hear her song and that she will arrive home not in the heavens where he himself awaits God triumphantly in snowstorms, but in the warm kingdom of the butterfly and the blossoms. I am borrowing this poem of Nijhoff, which according to Vestdijk is one of the most valuable products of modern Dutch poetry, in order to illustrate how much the problem which I enter into here belongs to our general cultural heritage. Somewhere in his *Stern der Erlösung*, Rosenzweig writes that you can recognize Greek metaphysics by the word "really". They sought what really existed behind the colorful diversity of visible phenomenon and this was always changeless

---

2. O.D. DUINTJER, *Over eros en transcendentie bij Plato*, in *Filosofie aan de grens* (ed. H.P. KUNNEMAN en T.G.W. OUDEMANS), Assen, 1992, p. 165.

3. PLATO, *Symposium*, 29e.

4. T. DE BOER, *De God van de filosofen en de God van Pascal*, Den Haag, 1991, p. 78, 116, 120.

and timeless being. The world in the foreground is merely appearance. It has cost modernity, which has awoken out of the dream of metaphysics, much effort to find its way back to the ordinary world.

Having said something about Plato, I now would like to mention briefly something about the other giant from ancient times: Aristotle. With him the honor of concrete reality is restored, but this, however, is only relative. A philosophy of historical reality, an understanding of the concrete person in a changing society, can learn little from him. *Sophia*, the highest form of knowledge in Aristotle, is concerned with insight into first principles and is so a contemplative form of knowledge apart from the empirical. In science, *epistèmè*, knowledge is sought of the lasting, general forms which apply to many individuals. Individual transitory things are not a subject for science, at least not in so far as they are transitory. Rather, the particular is accidental and contingent. This conviction is recorded in the famous adage: "scientia non est individuorum" (there is no science of the individual). This saying is encountered again in another famous book about the methodology of the social sciences[5].

If we look up "scientia" in the dictionary, we find as its meaning: knowledge, science, to understand. If this would not be possible for individuals, the human situation would be noticeably more miserable than it in fact is. The individual as individual would not even come up. Nor would it be able to be talked about. The subject which determines generalities is in any case a "conscious being" which is unable to express the reality of itself in its general pronouncements.

Applied to the example used in the beginning, this would mean that a science of the United States is possible, but not of the upper left brick in the facade of the Opera in Bozeman, Montana. Nevertheless, the imagination springs forth like a fountain when this topic is raised. Furthermore, the individual is not merely a subject for discussion; the individual also expresses oneself. When the student hands in the 5000 word essay she says to the teacher Phaedrus: "I was sitting in the hamburger restaurant across the street and began to write about the first stone, and the second stone, and by the third stone something broke through and I could not stop. It was if I was crazy. I was tormented by it, but here it is. I don't understand it".

Moreover, the teacher does not understand it. The cause of the incomprehension, according to me, lies in the tradition that I have just sketched which has taken this from us, but the means to understand this, but which at the same time cannot stop the experience. Even though it does not fit into the world view, the experience breaks through. This story also recounts, in a pleasant way, the manner in which a break through of a way of thinking can take place. The student remains blocked until the moment she can do no more. Once she receives the assignment to write about the

5. A.D. DE GROOT, *Methodologie*, Den Haag, 1964, p. 362.

one brick, she is confronted with a block. At that moment she can either allow it to make her mad, or throw off the traditional blinders. She does the latter and is then considered crazy by those around her. But for her it is a creative madness. People in this situation cannot understand each other. About such situations Wittgenstein says in *Über Gewissheit*: "Wo sich wirklich zwei Prinzipien treffen, die sich miteinander aussöhnen, da erklärt jeder den Anderen für einen Narren und Ketzer"[6].

If someone were now to ask me why it is that a culture is fixated first upon the universal, unchangeable and then only gradually – in fact since historicism – does a fascination with the individual and historic break through, I would have no answer. I could only observe that intellectual history has, in fact, evolved in such a way. What we could attempt is to assess the implications of this Western history for the subject with which we are here busy: the world of faith.

A recent example is the case of Levinas. When Levinas introduces his philosophy in the preface to *Totalité et Infini* he does so, in his own words, by contrasting "prophetic eschatology" against the "evidences of philosophy". Levinas wants to bring the insights from the prophetic tradition to bear upon philosophy. He is in this regard comparable to the Church Fathers who wanted to do the same with the truths of Christianity. What is striking is that even in the 20th century, Levinas appears to connect this formulation with the oldest tradition of philosophy: the opposition between evidence, or *epistèmè*, and opinion, or *doxa*. It is as if nothing has changed in more than 20 centuries. Those who would translate Jewish or Christian wisdom into Greek are unavoidably confronted with the opposition with which philosophy more or less began. The later Levinas, it is true, refers to another more modern conception of philosophy whereby facts can also be a source of rationality – he then expressly calls upon De Waelhens[7] – but I would like to save a discussion of this alternative for later. It is important for us first to realize the place "faith" – to use this expression for the time being – is assigned, almost as a matter of course, whenever it is confronted with a philosophy which is focused upon unchangeable being and upon rational truths which are eternal truths. Faith and prophecy belong to "opinion" which concerns the changeable and can produce only truths of facts, "vérité de faits".

In principle there is here defined, within this framework, the antithesis of faith and reason. And it has remained so through the centuries. The extent to which this is the case can be seen, for example, in some of the definitions of science upon which all theologians depend: science is knowledge which is certain, necessary and evident (Duns Scotus); a disposition of the soul used to establish a necessary property of a subject (Ockam); insight into the coherence of values, by means of irrefutable

---

6. L. WITTGENSTEIN, *Ueber Gewissheit*, Frankfurt am Main, 1971, p. 157.
7. E. LEVINAS, *Autrement qu'être ou au-delà de l'essence*, Den Haag, 1974, p. 24, 154.

deductions established from self-evident axioms (Reimarus). All this squares with the definition of Aristotle: science is the possibility of the human soul to establish certain truths concerning the general and the necessary[8].

Pascal rightly summarized this way of knowing under the term "esprit de géometrie" in so far as mathematics was the model of true knowledge for the Greeks. It concerned unchangeable entities, "numbers themselves", and ideal geometrical figures, and was seen to be based upon self-evidence.

2. The God of the Patriarchs and God as Being

Pascal's name needs to be mentioned here because he fought against the dominance of this view of knowledge and rejected its results in theology. D. Runia has recently demonstrated once more that the contrast between the God of the philosophers and the God of the Patriarchs is a much older tradition, without this necessarily leading directly to a conflict. Already Augustine, in his commentaries on Exodus 3, places the name of God in verse 14 – *ego sum qui sum* (I am who I am) – in opposition to the God of the Patriarchs in verse 15. God has an eternal name which indicates what he is in himself, and a temporary name which indicates what he is for humans. The first is *nomen incommutabilitatis* (a name of unchangeableness), the second is *nomen misericordiae* (a name of mercy). A comparable exegesis is found in the contemporary of Jesus, Philo of Alexandria. In verse 14 God says that he is being, which actually means that he has no name. God as being is not comprehensible by the intellect. But people, due to their weakness, need a name and therefore give God the name of the three Patriarchs. Runia sees Philo as the representative of a broader movement in which, for the first time, biblical tradition is brought into relation with the philosophical thinking of Greek and Hellenistic culture. This movement goes back at least to the translation of the Septuagint where God's name is translated as "ho oon", being.

Thus the contrast between the God of the philosophers and the God of the Patriarchs existed more than 15 centuries before Pascal addressed the topic. What is the meaning of the contrast here? According to Runia, Philo's contribution consists in the fact that he regarded the Platonic paradigm as the system of thought most appropriate for the explanation of the truth revealed to Moses. This paradigm is summarized by Runia as that of being and becoming, unchangeableness and changeableness, knowledge and ignorance. Runia partially agrees with Meijering when

---

8. See H.J. ADRIAANSE et al., *Het verschijnsel theologie*, Amsterdam-Meppel, 1987, p. 15, 21.

he sees unchangeability, the first name, as the philosophical expression of God's faithfulness. More important, according to Runia, is another conviction in Plato which is powerfully continued in the Church Fathers, the conviction of God's exaltedness or, said philosophically, God's transcendence. "God as he really is, is only known by himself." ... "God's essence is not accessible to humankind"[9].

From the Platonic paradigm it also follows that God's second name refers to becoming, changeableness and understandability. This is also the case in that the Patriarchs are temporary figures which appear in a history which we can comprehend. The question which we here want to ask concerns the theological implications of the Platonic paradigm. There should then be an opposition between the names of verse 14 and verse 15. This means that the second name is not actually God's name. The Church Father Basil says this expressly. If the second name is a name of mercy, as Augustine says, is this not a reflection of God's essence? And is one able to maintain, as Runia does, that the heart of the gospel is not affected by its Hellinization? Can unchangeable Being be merciful? Or is it so that God, out of compassion for the weakness and inadequacy of human knowing (Augustine), did reveal his essence in referring to the Patriarchs, and this revelation was as ... compassion. In other words, when God reveals himself in his relation with us, must that not be – if it is to be a genuine revelation – a revelation of how "he is in himself"? If God really wants to let himself be known, does he not let himself be known as he knows himself?

The same questions must be asked concerning exaltedness and transcendence. Would not God's transcendence consist precisely in his compassion? Is this compassion – rescuing a people in slavery from oppression – not exaltedness par excellence? Why would exaltedness consist in unchangeability? Why would we project an unreachable transcendent God above the God which reveals himself?

Perhaps one might want to answer the last question with: because we also want to philosophize. We do not want to remain with pure faith in revelation. We want to *express* our faith *philosophically*. Then I would like to pose the question: what do we gain by expressing trustworthiness as unchangeability? That this philosophical expression is understandable by all, and not just by believers? But should trustworthiness not best be expressed by "trustworthiness"? What is so unphilosophical about trustworthiness? Why would this be less understood than unchangeableness? What sense does it make to explain trustworthiness to intellectuals as unchangeability when intellectuals who do not understand changeability and who do understand unchangeability no longer exist? This situation raises the question: what do we understand today as philosophy? What

---

9. D.H.T. RUNIA, *Platonisme, Philonisme en het begin van het christelijk denken*, Utrecht, 1992, p. 23 ff.

do we wish philosophy to add to our expression of faith?

I know that these are unhistorical questions. It is certainly not my intention, as Adriaanse suggests[10], to ban the early Church Fathers to the underworld because of their philosophy. I agree with Runia that the process of Hellenization was not necessary; it could have been otherwise. According to me, it makes sense to speculate on how it could have been different (according to Weber, this is the only way to understand something in history). It makes no sense to blame the first Christians on this account; certainly not if one would have undoubtedly made the same choices oneself. The real question then is whether we in the 20th century, now that the era of metaphysics has come to an end, must *continue* with such an approach. Are there not, as Adriaanse himself says[11], reasons "to become nervous" about the results of cohabitation? Can we in theology still act as if the message of Nietzsche's "toller Mensch" does not concern us? Have Pascal, Hamann and Kierkegaard warned us to no avail? Must we continue to hold these free spirits prisoner in our Christian-metaphysical Orcus? The argument that, in our break with the metaphysics of being, we saw off the branch upon which we sit, does not hold water, since the branch is already broken. We have been hovering or falling for a long time now (granted with "verneinende Gebärde").

In the meantime the question remains concerning whether or not there is an opposition contained in Exodus 14 and Exodus 15. What is intended with God's being named "I am who I am"? Rosenzweig, who with Buber translated the Hebrew *ehjeh asjer ehjeh* as "Ich werde dasein, als der ich dasein werde", wrote on this topic: "Mit sein geht es nicht. Das ist im Deutschen hoffnungslos platonisiert, wie in allen nachplatonischen Sprachen, dass mittelarterliche Hebräisch nicht ausgenommen. Wir wollen doch nicht die Abscheulichkeiten der Septuaginta weitergeben"[12]. Rozenzweig gives evidence of his agreement with Rasji who paraphrases: "Ich bin mit ihnen in dieser Not, wie ich mit ihnen sein werde in der Slaverei der übrigen Fremdherrschaften" (with this last the slavery in Babylon and Rome would be intended). Here the concern is not with the absolute being of God in himself but with his presence among people. The first name means the same as the second; the opposition disappears.

What can be said here concerning the Hebrew text? Recently two articles have appeared on this question which both point in the same

10. H.J. ADRIAANSE, *Met God zonder God*, in *De God van de filosofen en de God van de Bijbel*, Zoetermeer, 1991, p. 83.

11. IDEM, *Four Reasons to Become Nervous and Two Possible Remedies*, in *Christian Faith and Philosophical Theology*, Kampen, 1992.

12. F. ROSENZWEIG, *Der Mensch und sein Werk, Gesammelte Schriften*, Part 4, Volume 2: *Sprachdenken – die Schrift*, Dordrecht, 1984, p. 93 f.

direction[13]. Because, according to me, the Hebrew is the decisive factor, I will summarize it here. According to Van der Wal *ehjeh* points to the future and to a relation which is made clear in verse 12. Furthermore, *ehjeh* in verse 14b is a proper name. If we take *asjer* as a conjunction, then the expression *ehjeh asjer ehjeh* can be translated: "EHJEH, because I will be there". Van de Wal sees the expression as a summary of the line in the Psalm: "It is he who offers us his friendship". Beentjes adds to this that *asjer* cannot be seen as a relative pronoun because *ehjeh* needs to have the same meaning in both clauses due to the parallel construction. A relative pronoun would give to the first *ehjeh* the function of a copula. "To be" is really a verb; it points to an occurrence, a being-present. The repetition indicates an emphasis. Beentjes proposes the translation: "I am with you regardless". The "name pronouncement" occurs at the beginning of the stories about the exodus from Egypt and the journey through the desert, a period in which God's redeeming presence would manifest itself par excellence.

The lesson we can learn from this historical excursus, in my opinion, is two-fold. First, that an opposition between the God of the philosophers (in the Platonic sense) and that of the Patriarchs in the Hebrew Bible does not occur at all, and second, that the introduction of such an opposition into the text causes an ambiguity which complicates and obscures the intention. One question which now presents itself is: why is philosophy necessary? Why does Jewish wisdom need to be translated into Greek? We will see that this question allows two different answers.

Before I continue, I would like to make one remark in order to prevent misunderstanding. The influence of the identification of the God of the Bible with the being of Greek philosophy has been tremendous. I refer here to the study of Cornelia de Vogel *Antike Seinsphilosophie und Christentum im Wandel der Jahrhunderte*[14]. It is not the case that the Reformation broke with this tradition. In the classic work of reformed Protestantism, the *Gereformeerde Dogmatiek* of H. Bavinck, when the theory of God is discussed, for example the unchangeability or the independence (aseitas) of God, we find the same sentence as refrain: "the Reformation brought with it no change here"[15]. What we are talking about here is a communal inheritance and thus a communal challenge.

13. A.J.O. VAN DER WAL, '*Hij is het, die ons Zijne vriendschap biedt*', Ex. 3:14 nog-maals gelezen, Ter Herkenning, 19 (1991) 109 ff.; P.C. BEENTJES, De vertaling van drie cruciale woorden in Exodus 3,14, Ibidem, 115 ff.

14. C.J. DE VOGEL, Antike Seinsphilosophie und Christentum im Wandel der Jahrhunderte, Baden-Baden, 1958.

15. H. BAVINCK, Gereformeerde dogmatiek, II, Kampen, 1918, p. 14, 95, 139.

3. The Rise of the Philosophy of Life: phronèsis

I spoke in the beginning about the oldest philosophical tradition wherein the opposition of *ratio* and *opinio*, of eternal truth and factual truth, is contained. Given the stubbornness with which this question continues to exist, one might ask where in the history of philosophy the most important break occurs. It is usually in the rise of modern mathematical natural sciences that a break with classical thinking is seen. Here with the help of mathematics, which until now had been considered an art, a genuine science of the changeable comes into being. There came into being a new type of science as well which was focused upon control and which brought forth technology, a technology which would, as Weber once said, unrecognizably change, not only the face of the earth but also the face of humankind.

Yet there are also arguments that support seeing the most important break not in the rise of natural science but in the historical sciences of the 19th century. Whitehead showed that it was entirely possible to interpret the natural sciences in an old metaphysical framework. In the mechanistic philosophy of nature, according to Whitehead, logical constructions of a highly abstract character were erected in the place of concrete reality. He called it the fallacy of misplaced concreteness. The abstract is interpreted as concrete and taken as true reality, which at the same time then serves to disqualify the concretely appearing world as mere appearance. An old metaphysical pattern of thinking returns, now supported by the new natural sciences. From Galileo on, the properties of quantitative mass and simple location were considered as essential. Other properties did not "actually" exist. Regardless whether one saw light as particles or as waves, common to both theories is that light or color does not really occur in reality. And the same goes for sound and smell. We must not, as Whitehead puts it, give nature the credit which is due ourselves. It is we who produce the smell of the rose and the song of the nightingale and then project it onto nature, a nature which in fact consists of particles and waves. The poets get it wrong when they sing of nature. Their point of departure is the popular *doxa*, the appearance of the senses. The philosopher knew better, but the natural sciences can now scientifically demonstrate it: "Nature is a dull affair, soundless, scentless, colorless; merely the hurrying of material, endlessly, meaninglessly"[16]. The bees thus are right in fleeing the world in the desire for higher honey.

It is interesting to note that someone like Windelband, who proposes an ideographic method for history where in the individual and the particular is described, gives a completely metaphysical interpretation to the natural sciences. He writes that the goal of the natural sciences, however

---

16. A.N. WHITEHEAD, *Science and the Modern World*, New York, 1925, p. 54.

clear their point of departure might be, is in the final analysis mathematical formulations of laws of movement: "they leave behind – genuinely Platonic – the individual, sensually perceivable thing which comes into being and which perishes, and consider such as appearances without essence, in order to pursue knowledge of the systematic necessities which govern occurrences in timeless unchangeability"[17]. He calls that a triumph of thinking over perception. We are here still in the grip of Parmenides and Plato.

On the basis of the above I am inclined to see in the 19th century rise of historicism and the philosophy of life a deeper break in the history of philosophy than was the case with the Enlightenment. Even with someone like Locke, who is seen as an empiricist, mathematics is still the model of all knowledge. In Kant the ideal of rational a priori knowledge lives on in the idea of a priori synthetic truth which is inventoried and systematized in the "System der Grundsätze". Husserl correctly calls it an ontology of nature. He saw in it an example of his own regional ontologies which had a much wider scope and were to include the entire life world, and at the same time were also the continuation of a very old tradition. Also Heidegger can, in a certain sense, be connected here when he at first links the question of being with these ontologies. He even speaks, in the beginning of *Sein und Zeit,* of the "ontological preference" of the question of being. Nevertheless, a radical change is also implied here because regional ontology can only be correctly understood from the perspective of the question of being: not as a doctrine about ideal "Gegenstande" but as a making more explicit of temporal ways to beings, as open horizons, which we have always travelled before we caught sight of Being. In addition, Heidegger stresses that the ontological explications always have their roots in ontic experiences. The latter reveals the change which Dilthey brought about: here, fact is a source of rationality or a source of meaning. Heidegger therefore talks about an hermeneutic of facticity. This term can also be rightly used for the work of Levinas. He too asks the meaning of certain facts – and then in such a way that they trespass the frame of existential ontology: redemption, a state of being hostage[18].

The philosophy of life of Dilthey does not imply that life is hostile to ideas and reflection. This might be called real irrationalism, in as much as it turns rationalism around. This is the case for certain vitalists such as Klages, and in a certain sense also Nietzsche. In Dilthey, life demands awakening in language and concepts. In this respect philosophy can be compared to poetry. Ida Gerhardt says in her first published poem that one's own life is, driving and steady, a hidden laboring "until the deepest

---

17. W. WINDELBAND, *Präludien II*, Tübingen, ⁸1921, p. 151.

18. T. DE BOER, *Van Brentano tot Levinas*, Amsterdam-Meppel, 1989, p. 92, 102 ff., 157.

desire comes to rest in the word".

Dilthey wants to show that it is possible to grasp life in a concept. In the traditional theory of abstraction, which descends from Aristotle, the particular is impenetrable in the forming of a concept. Concepts are always universals which refer to general characteristics.

The "sinister individual", as De Rijk says, is a challenger and a killjoy of thinking, but cannot itself be grasped in a concept[19]. Organizing and understanding the particular will always be at the expense of that which is unique to the individual. Yet Pascal has already foreseen an alternative in his "esprit de finesse", a way of knowing which agrees with everyday knowledge and at the same time sees both the totality and the detail. In fact Pascal already formulates the essence of the hermeneutic circle here. The "esprit de finesse" is the spirit of interpretation, the key notion of the new humanities[20].

Yet, it is not Pascal's "esprit de finesse" but the notion of "phronesis", found in Aristotle's *Nichomachean Ethics*, which was destined to play an historic role by breaking open the model of knowledge which stemmed from that same Aristotle. The concept was brought to light in the earlier lectures of Heidegger and later it played a key role in Gadamer's hermeneutics. For in the notion of "phronesis" we find the three characteristics needed in order to understand people and historic cultures. First of all, it is a knowledge which concerns us; it is relevant for our practical life. So the famous gap between theory and practice is stopped here in advance. Second, it is knowledge of the particular. And third, there is always an indirect relation with ethics. According to Aristotle there is a difference between someone we call prudent in particular cases, and an opportunist. I am not aware of whether or not Pascal saw any relation between "phronesis" and "esprit de finesse". In Aristotle, "phronesis" concerns exclusively human cases, but in principle it is possible to widen that form of knowledge to the "nicht daseinsmaszige" beings, to use Heidegger's words. Our example about the first brick in the upper left corner of the Opera is in the theory of abstraction purely a carrier of the universal being brick – all bricks are then the same and equally interesting or uninteresting. Aristotle's philosophy of nature, however, allows one to see the brick as a *minimum naturale*. *Minima naturalia* are different from atoms because they differ qualitatively and specifically (as was still the case in Empedocles) and because they allow changes and not only differences in external configuration[21]. Seen in this way, this brick catches the eye as an object of interest and so does

19. *Ibidem.*

20. T. DE BOER, *De God van de filosofen en de God van Pascal* (n. 4), p. 128, 136 f.

21. A.G.M. VAN MELSEN, *De geschiedenis van het begrip atoom*, Utrecht-Antwerpen, 1962, p. 60ff., 69f. 82ff., 95; *The Philosophy of Nature of Andreas G.M. van Melsen*, in *Geloven in de wereld. Een vriendenboek voor en over prof. dr. A.G.M. van Melsen*, 1985, Nijmegen, p. 122 f.

the second brick. There is a painting by Magritte "The Empty Frame" in which brick after brick "comes up" in that way.

Dilthey, however, primarily focuses on the human being. He is the first to try to find an alternative for a generalizing, explanatory psychology and he introduces the notion "life cohesion". Later he particularly focuses on the analysis of objective meanings which result in works of culture. A product of civilization is always a singular unity with its own unique identity and style, like Magritte's painting. In the interpretation, this complex of meaning is articulated and analyzed, also in it's structural moments. This is an undertaking which never ends because each great work requires an ongoing interpretation.

According to Heidegger, it is not enough only to set the historic against the non-historic. He criticizes this opposition of the historic and the ontic, in the terminology of York von Wartenburg, or of the existential and the categorial in his own terms, because there is a more original perspective: that of being. Existence and reality are both ways of being, a being which unlocks the "da" and is therefore called "daseinsmaszig" and a being which shines in that light and which we have called "thing" until now. From the point of view of being as halo of the "da" — in traditional language, Heidegger calls this the "genus" from which the "ontic" and the "historic" originate as specifications — the concept of thing of the tradition has to be broken down and be reconstructed. We could call this a kind of "phronesis" of nature, of the "not daseinsmaszige" beings. The individual brick I mentioned before loses its eternity — that means for it, its eternal oblivion — and becomes a living brick again. The thing is no longer a simple *res extensa* which is taken up in a causal series, but can be marked by the "esprit de finesse" as a crystallization point of a world view. So the brick still has a function in the Psalms and in the first letter of Peter.

With this turning of the philosophy of life, an alternative is created to classical metaphysics, a paradigm in which time, fact and story play a key role. What does that mean for Jewish or Christian wisdom looking to be translated into Greek, that is, looking for philosophical expression?

Against the background of this philosophy of life, we need to read the passage in the article "God and Philosophy" in which Levinas disputes the opposition between the God of the philosophers and the God of the Fathers, which stems from Halevi and is adopted by Pascal. It is not because this contrast does not exist, but rather, because it is no longer a dilemma. Levinas explicitly says that we do not have to chose between the reasonableness of philosophy and the opinions of faith. There is a third possibility[22]. Faith has its own reasonableness; there is a "rational discourse which is not ontology, nor language of faith". Levinas calls

---

22. *God en de filosofie*, translated, introduced and provided with notes by T. DE BOER, Den Haag, 1990, p. 13.

this "rationality or rationalism (sic!) of transcendence" (la rationalité et le rationalisme de la transcendance). In other words, prophecy has its own philosophy. Levinas' whole effort aims to give philosophical expression to the pre-philosophic experience of prophetism. This is the way from prophecy to philosophy. Along this way one can be a philosopher without leaving prophecy or in other words, remain loyal to the prophetic tradition without rejecting philosophy.

The combination of biblical tradition with Greek metaphysics of being has become so self evident in Christianity that a rejection of this metaphysics might simply be interpreted as a rejection of philosophy itself. One would then have to be satisfied with faith alone, and in that sense be a "fideist". Peter Jonkers, for example, writes of my view: "his rejection of traditional metaphysics and natural theology is so radical that he makes every philosophical approach to God, how hesitant and not-objectivating it might be, impossible"[23]. This reasoning is only true if philosophy coincides with traditional metaphysics and with natural theology. Using Luther's words, it seems that for faith only "Hure Vernunft" is available and that there is no other more attractive partner: the rationalism of transcendence. There is an alternative. In a scheme it could be reproduced like this:

1. esprit de géometrie   3. The God of Philosophy
2. esprit de finesse   4. The God of the Bible

Throughout history, the choice has always been for the cohabitation of 1 and 4 which has resulted in the mixture which we discussed in the historical section 2: the coalition of a rational, natural knowledge of God and biblical theology (the combination of 3 and 4), the product of which Pascal disputes: The God of the philosophers. Yet he leaves the combination of 2 and 4 open. What is more, many of his ideas in the *Pensées* are the connection of biblical thinking with "esprit de finesse". I understand the passages about human restlessness — from distraction to warfare — with which he pushes aside the original experience of meaninglessness, precisely as that search for "points of connection with the religious question of meaning", something Jonkers cannot find with me, although I try to follow Pascal in this.

---

23. P. JONKERS, *Filosofie*, in *Handboek godsdienst in Nederland* (ed. H. SCHAEFFER), Amersfoort, 1992, p. 252.

4. Why Philosophy?

In the next part of this article we will try to find the answer to two questions: Why does prophecy need philosophy? And, What does such a philosophy look like in concrete? The first question requires a double answer. The need for philosophy stems primarily from the necessity for confrontation. In its environment, Jewish wisdom (and later Christian) encounters philosophy and has to justify itself with respect to it. The love of wisdom had already taken a certain form in the dominant culture and ruled the intellectual elite. With respect to this a position had to be worked out. In the twentieth century, in the coming of the Jewish Renaissance, it is no different. Levinas, who had been brought up with the Jewish Scriptures, encounters modern philosophy chiefly in the form of phenomenology. From the very beginning, however, he is dissatisfied with this way of thinking. The confrontation at first takes the shape of an "ethically transcendental-philosophy". The evidences of philosophy are taken as the point of departure, and from this point of departure one tries to go back and interrogate a deeper experience which does not get discussed in that same philosophy, although such an experience must be assumed as a kind of foundation or ferment.

Gradually, however, Levinas develops his own philosophy with his own "system" of categories (a "system" which is not a real system but rather a text, of which the components are the contexts for each other; the deductive coherence makes place for an internal, hermeneutic one). These basic principles are the result of experiences which, according to him, "have to become thoughts": the experience of a kidnapping, of the responsibility for freedom, of one-for-the-other. Why do these experiences have to be thought? Because these experiences require reflection, explanation, interpretation and discussion in an intellectual-philosophical culture. That is the way from prophecy to philosophy that I have already spoken about (in the scheme of section 3: from 4 to 2).

In this context we also need to say something about the relation between Levinas' Jewish and his philosophical writings. Often it is explained as if it is the believer speaking to fellow believers in the former and the philosopher who speaks based upon reason to all people in the latter. But then one forgets that the content of the philosophical writings are exactly the same as the Jewish ones[24]. So it is not true that in the two, different sources of knowledge are being used. Then we are guilty of projecting a scheme upon Levinas' way of thinking which is not true. Rather we encounter a difference in the level of expression: one of direct colloquial language and one of philosophical reflection. Although I have not researched this, I dare to introduce the hypothesis that, with respect

24. T. DE BOER, *Tussen filosofie en profetie*, Baarn, 1988, p. 85; IDEM, *Van Brentano tot Levinas*, p. 151 ff.

to content, the convictions of Levinas can first be found in his Jewish writings and later in his philosophical ones. As a result, accordingly, he goes from prophecy to philosophy.

Finally I would like to make the remark that the shift in Levinas' position is also a natural development. Thinking concerning the particular is only started by the shock which comes from the other. The initial contact will especially be a confrontation in the sense that one is looking for openings in a thinking with totalitarian pretentions. Once one's own thinking is in movement and is better articulated, then it will attempt to make the other, which was at first threatening, part of one's own thinking.

How radically Levinas has taken a distance from onto-theology appears especially in his already mentioned "God and Philosophy". Shortly after Levinas published this article, he received an honorary doctorate in Leiden. I remember him commenting upon it in Heering's house: "c'est calme". The philosophy of prophecy found its ultimate expression in that piece. But that does not mean that there is not a hot discussion going on within it. The foundations of Western thinking are thoroughly uprooted in it. There is no other text in which he used such fundamental arguments concerning transcendence. The expression "rationality of transcendence" which he uses here, gets its full weight when we realize that the rationality of ontotheology is a rationality of *immanence*. In classical Western ontology the notion of transcendence can not be thought at all.

The article starts with the remark: "Western philosophical discourse claims to be the all-embracing frame and the final horizon for understanding". Consequently, it states that rational theology has accepted this "bondage". We could ask ourselves whether Philo and Augustine thoroughly realized what they were doing when they introduced the Highest Being into theology? It was meant as an homage to God's incomprehensibility and inaccessibility. Many Christian theologians have done the same. Luther thought that behind the God of Revelation there was the dark and hidden background of the *deus absconditus*. One could learn from philosophy that God is incomprehensible and that the human being is "non capax infiniti". H. Bavinck still express himself this way in his *Gereformeerde dogmatiek*. He emphasizes the value of that incomprehensability in the face of those who want to stick with revelation[25]. Through the philosophers, we learn the majesty and greatness of God. Together with Barth we could ask ourselves whether this magnificence is not precisely to be found in his servanthood[26]. I, however, would like to point out something else with respect to this. God as highest being was not without reason a God of philosophers. He was God, known through the *logos* or the *ratio*. Could Christian theologians have guessed that rational

25. H. Bavinck, *Gereformeerde dogmatiek*, II (n. 15), p. 14, 16, 21, 113.
26. T. de Boer, *De God van de filosofen en de God van Pascal* (n. 4), p. 84.

theology would gradually monopolize rationality? One has to understand very well that for philosophers, Being is par excellence the thing to be known. According to Parmenides, Being and thinking are the same. Plato states in his *Politeia* that what is complete, is completely knowable (*to men panteloos on panteloos gnooston*)[27]. For philosophers, it is not the unchangeable that is incomprehensible, but the changeable. Time has always been considered as non-being and unknowable. When the patriarchs say: God can not be known with respect to his Being, but is comprehensible with respect to his revelation, they turn it around. This is probably an indication of how much they took God's revelation in time for granted based upon his deeds. In dogmatics one speaks of communicable and incommunicable characteristics[28]. It is, however, the incommunicable characteristics — independence (aseitas), unity, eternity, omnipresence, unchangeability (I'll come back to this later) — which are considered thinkable in philosophy. The communicable characteristics, on the other hand — reason, will, power — are rejected in philosophy as anthropomorphisms. So the thinking of the *logos* has an imperial style. If something at all is left over from revelation, then it must be irrational doctrines, typically something for faith, the organ with which you can apparently accept what you cannot know. *Ratio* can be compared better with a concubine, who slowly gets rid of the partner with whom she is living, than with a whore (Luther).

I hope that by now it has become clear that there are different answers possible to the question: "why do we need philosophy?" An answer which enslaves us and an answer which liberates us from that slavery.

5. From Prophecy to Philosophy

Those who have followed me up until now will probably make the remark that the kind of philosophy for which I ask, namely a reflection upon the meaning-founding facts of the Christian tradition, has already existed for a long time and this in the shape of Christian theology. With this I return to the already mentioned question concerning what philosophy in fact is understood to mean. What are our expectations with respect to it? If there is no intention to reduce true facts to rational ones — which was still the platform of the Enlightenment — but rather to explain what local happenings mean for those who live in time (and that is, in my opinion, the essence of the crisis of religion: we no longer know what the facts of salvation mean for our existence), then, I think that the entire traditional distinction between theology and philosophy disappears. All traditions which have something to say about the meaning of our exis-

27. PLATO, *De staat*, 477 a 2-4.
28. H. BAVINCK, *Gereformeerde dogmatiek*, II (n. 15), p. 113, 117, 137 ff., 171 ff.

tence, which are, using Ricoeur's words, "propositions de sens", are principally on the same level. Of course there is also hard science, but that is no competitor. It is *hors concours* because in principal it does not raise the question of meaning.

For the last part of my article, I would like to return to the beginning. We have seen that according to the Anti-Phaedrus from Pirsig's book we have to descend the pyramid of being in order to reach inspiring concrete reality. In my opinion, theology also should descend this ladder, from the top of the universe all the way down. But it must also go up again. My ladder is therefore a typical Jacob's ladder, which can be used to go up and down. As far as I am concerned, you can even use the words of Heraclitus: the way down is the way up. But, first the way down must be taken in order to go up again in a responsible way. In the phenomenology of Husserl and Heidegger we have learned that a construction must always precede a destruction. Husserl thought that he could execute the first movement in one step, by means of an epoché. Heidegger has taught us that instead it must be patient historical research, although he himself speaks very radically about a "Destruktion aller bisherigen Ontologie".

1. The negative movement of theology, the way down, in my view, is a reconstruction of the *history of dogma*. Personally I am against simply abolishing dogmas. Dogmas need not be accepted or rejected, but rather explained. Dogmas can be seen as an excerpt or extract of narratives. We become guilty of the fallacy of misplaced concreteness when we see them as descriptions. In the explanation, the relation with the narrative foundation has to be restored. I consider the work of Schillebeeckx such a reconstruction. I see his work as an attempt to reduce abstract notions in dogmatics to their narrative basis, thus paralleling Husserl's attempt to anchor the ideas of natural science again in the social environment. Schillebeeckx speaks about predicates of reflection of the first and second degree which originated in the concrete experience with the historic Jesus. So we take a few steps down again. I have never understood the magisterium's disapproval of this undertaking, because it happens in order to save the dogma, not to pull it to pieces. Here dogma is once again turned upside down; it becomes a building of living bricks.

An example of what I think this reconstruction represents, is the rewriting of the conflict concerning the relation between the kerygmatic Christ and the historic Jesus. This controversy appears in a totally different light when we do not describe this opposition according to the Platonic (in fact a geometric) model of eidos and fact, or of idea and example, (or of rational and factual truth) – a view which always ends up in a misunderstanding of the historical facts – but according to the model of the meaning giving fact and the unfolding interpretation of that fact. In the latter model the meaning of the fact is disclosed in the explanation.

Only during and after the explanation do we know what the fact means, and so what the fact was. Gadamer rightly calls this process of interpretation a "Seinszuwachs"; something is added. But what is added to the explanation afterwards is not a projection which is put over the facts like a bell jar, like the *Leben Jesu Forschung* thought, and which can later be exposed as deceit. The interpretation shows something which was already there before we saw it. There lays a rationality in the facts themselves, as De Waelhens argues[29]. The more concentrated this original experience was, the more time its processing requires. In fact, the interpretation determines what the actual fact means for us, but that cannot be used against what it originally was. It is quite normal, with respect to historical judgments, that only after years, sometimes after centuries, do we specify what something means, what it actually was. The historical Jesus stands in fact at the beginning but just as well at the end.

2. After this way down, there is also a way back up and here philosophy also plays an important role, and does not deserve to be treated as a discipline to which theology should be opposed. There is indeed a task for philosophy, even if we start with the God of the Bible, or in other words, after the deconstruction of the God of the philosophers. In that way up I see three steps.

a. In the first place, a foundation is formed by exegeses and biblical theology. Here the narrative basis is marked out and inventoried. My reflection on Ex 3,14-15 has accentuated how important this research is. It is striking how much light is thrown upon the text or how much meaning is exuded when the platonic-metaphysical frame is removed.

b. The second step, in my opinion, is reflection on the basic biblical notions with respect to their content. These things used to come up for discussion under the chapter on the characteristics of God. What seems interesting to me in modern theology is how the biblical notions, such as omnipotence, unchangeability and independence (aseitas) are attempted to be re-thought. This is the "thinking" which Levinas also seeks. "Il faut penser" is a recurring refrain in his writings. I would like to make a remark about some of those notions as an example. According to the doctrine of the unchangeability of God, we can have a relation with God, but not God with us.

I do not need to borrow this position from Thomas because it also appears in the already mentioned Bavinck. "Absolute being is, because it is. The notion of God spontaneously brings with it unchangeability", we read in the latter. "There is change around him and outside of him, there is change in the relation with him, but there is no change in God

29. See A. DE WAELHENS, *La philosophie et les expériences naturelles*, Den Haag, 1961, p. 36 ff.

himself"[30]. If absolute being is not, because it is, but only is because it receives a meaning in time, then that brings with it, to continue my logic, God's changeability. But then what does eternity mean? We cannot do without that concept. I suspect that it has something to do with reliability. Something that is really good, survives the decline which is part of each *gloria mundi*. It really is "something permanent down here".

The characteristic of *aseitas*, independence, has still greater problems than unchangeability, all the more when it is related to happiness. As it appeared in a dissertation about *Deus immutabilis*, happiness in the greatest possible amount is unique to God. He cannot grieve. "He only enjoys. He cannot suffer: his happiness is not susceptible to decrease nor is it to intensification. And that because he and his happiness are independent from everything outside of him, in other words from creatures. God is most satisfactory to himself and therefore most happy"[31]. It is said so simply and sounds rather orthodox: "He cannot suffer". I think that this is very heretical. Strasser once said that God needed a body in order to be able to suffer. That is the meaning of Incarnation. I also believe that Paul Moyaert is right when he writes that we have arrived in a sadistic universe with this doctrine of happiness[32].

c. I see the third step as a typically philosophical one, the reflection on central philosophical categories: for example, fact, time and story. I have already given an example of how much of a role notions such as time, fact, idea and example play, unreflectively, in discussion about the historical Jesus. It could be a task unique to philosophy – to point out some distribution of work between theologians and philosophers – to submit those key notions, abstracting from their concrete content, to closer research. In the philosophical tradition, fact is not only opposed to *ratio* but also to norm. You cannot distill prescriptions from facts. Yet facts which create meaning are a source of orientation. This is also a reason to "think" this notion "fact" again, just like the contrasting notions of norm, activity and truth.

Nevertheless, however far we may ascend in philosophical reflection, we always have to be cautious to the fact that we cannot find Christian truth at the top of the universe, not on the back of heaven but, in contrast to what Plato thought, related to flesh and color. The facts which must be thought about most are incarnation, cross, revelation and the descent of the Holy Spirit. We cannot find them by ascending to the top of the universe. Instead they form, using a term from Husserl, the lowest "individuell Einzelheiten" in the hierarchy of beings, as he describes them

30. H. BAVINCK, *Gereformeerde dogmatiek*, II (n. 15), p. 147.

31. P. DEN OTTOLANDER, *Deus Immutabilis*, Assen, 1965, pp. 71-4, 75 ff.

32. P. MOYAERT, *Theologie, antropologie en theodicee*, in *Wijsgerig perpectief*, 30 (1989/90) 86. A theodicy is "the theoretical fiction or phantasmatic production in which one goes to any length in the affirmation that everything that is, that means even suffering, is good, delightful and meaningful somewhere for someone".

in the first section of *Ideas*. Dondeyne, the one after whom this chair is named, invented the wonderful term "fait primitif" for this. Theology and philosophy together make an effort in the ascertaining of what the meaning of this might be.

De Boelelaan 1105   T. DE BOER
NL-1081 HV Amsterdam

PERSONALIA

Lieven Boeve is Aspirant of the Belgian National Fund for Scientific Research, and Assistant of the Department of Dogmatic Theology at the Faculty of Theology, K.U. Leuven.

Theo De Boer is Professor of Philosophy at the Vrije Universiteit Amsterdam.

Joël Delobel is Dean of the Faculty of Theology at the K.U. Leuven and Professor of Exegesis.

Georges De Schrijver s.j. is Professor of Fundamental Dogmatic Theology, at the Department of Dogmatic Theology, Faculty of Theology, K.U. Leuven.

Herman-Emiel Mertens is Emeritus Professor of Dogmatic Theology and former President of the Department of Dogmatic Theology, Faculty of Theology, K.U. Leuven.

Antoon Vergote is Emeritus Professor of Psychology and Philosophy of Religion, K.U. Leuven.

INDEX OF AUTHORS

ANNUA NUNTIA LOVANIENSIA
LEUVEN UNIVERSITY PRESS – UITGEVERIJ PEETERS

Available: